Vietnamese Kitchen Guide

Blane .B Delgado

All rights reserved. Copyright © 2023 Blane .B Delgado

COPYRIGHT © 2023 Blane .B Delgado

All rights reserved.

No part of this book must be reproduced, stored in a retrieval system, or shared by any means, electronic, mechanical, photocopying, recording, or otherwise, without written permission from the publisher.

Every precaution has been taken in the preparation of this book; still the publisher and author assume no responsibility for errors or omissions. Nor do they assume any liability for damages resulting from the use of the information contained herein.

Legal Notice:

This book is copyright protected and is only meant for your individual use. You are not allowed to amend, distribute, sell, use, quote or paraphrase any of its part without the written consent of the author or publisher.

Introduction

Vietnamese cuisine is a vibrant tapestry of flavors, colors, and textures, reflecting the rich culinary heritage of this diverse and culturally rich country. In this cookbook, we invite you to explore the intoxicating world of classic Vietnamese street food, right in the comfort of your own home.

At the heart of Vietnamese cuisine lies an exquisite balance of flavors—sweet, savory, sour, and spicy—combined with fresh herbs and aromatic spices. From fragrant herbs like mint and cilantro to the fiery kick of chili peppers, each dish is a symphony of tastes that will tantalize your taste buds and transport you to the bustling streets of Vietnam.

Our journey through the flavors of Vietnam begins with an exploration of rolls, a quintessential street food found in every corner of the country. From fresh spring rolls bursting with crunchy vegetables and succulent shrimp to savory fried rolls filled with fragrant herbs and tender meats, these recipes capture the essence of Vietnamese cuisine in every bite.

Next, we delve into the world of Vietnamese salads, where fresh ingredients come together to create light and refreshing dishes that are perfect for any occasion. From tangy green papaya salad to vibrant herb salads bursting with flavor, these recipes showcase the incredible diversity of Vietnamese culinary traditions.

No Vietnamese meal would be complete without a selection of flour- and starch-based foods, from delicate dumplings to crispy pancakes. In this section, you'll find recipes for classic dishes like banh xeo, crispy Vietnamese pancakes filled with shrimp and bean sprouts, as well as banh cuon, delicate rice flour rolls stuffed with savory fillings.

Of course, no exploration of Vietnamese cuisine would be complete without a steaming bowl of noodle soup, or pho. In this section, we'll show you how to create the perfect bowl of pho at home, from the rich and aromatic broth to the tender slices of beef and chewy rice noodles.

For a comforting and nourishing meal, look no further than Vietnamese porridge, or chao. Made from rice simmered until soft and creamy, chao is a staple of Vietnamese comfort food, often served with an array of flavorful toppings like shredded chicken, crispy shallots, and fresh herbs.

For a lighter option, rice vermicelli noodles are the perfect choice. In this section, we'll show you how to prepare these delicate noodles and pair them with a variety of fresh vegetables, grilled meats, and zesty sauces to create delicious and satisfying meals.

Of course, no Vietnamese meal would be complete without a generous serving of rice, the cornerstone of Vietnamese cuisine. From fragrant jasmine rice to sticky glutinous rice, we'll show you how to cook rice perfectly every time and pair it with a variety of flavorful dishes.

Finally, no Vietnamese meal would be complete without a selection of refreshing drinks and sweet treats to round out the experience. From creamy Vietnamese iced coffee to refreshing fruit smoothies and decadent desserts, these recipes are the perfect way to end any meal on a sweet note.

So join us on a culinary adventure through the vibrant streets of Vietnam as we explore the rich tapestry of flavors, colors, and textures that make Vietnamese cuisine truly unforgettable. With our collection of classic Vietnamese street food recipes, you'll discover that the heart and soul of Vietnam can be found right in your own kitchen.

Contents

THE FLAVORS OF VIETNAM 1
ROLLS 28
    Peanut Soy Sauce Dip 35
    Shrimp and Pork Rice 37
    Vegan Fresh Rolls *Gỏi* 40
    Fried Pork and Egg 42
    Grilled / Roasted 48
    Pan-Seared Beef With 50
    Grilled Beef in Wild 52
    Roasted Fish With 54
SALADS 58
    Fish Sauce Salad 61
    Shrimp and Mango 62
    Green Papaya Salad 64
    Chicken and Cabbage 66
    Chicken and Onion 68
    Kohlrabi and Carrot 70
    Shrimp and Pomelo 72
    Banana Blossom 75
    Pan-Seared Beef and 81
    King Oyster 83
    Cucumber and Tofu 85
FLOUR- AND STARCH-BASED FOODS 88
    Crispy Savory Crêpes 95
    Chicken Curry BáNH 97
    Vegan Curry BáNh MÌ 100
    Baguette With Beef in 102
    Homemade 105
    Carrot and Daikon 106
    Grilled Pork Bánh Mì 108

- Grilled Chicken Bánh 110
- Pineapple Shrimp Bánh 112
- Char Siu Pork Bánh Mì 115

NOODLE SOUP 118
- Chicken PhO Salad *Phở* 133
- Red Wine Beef Stew 137

PORRIDGE 140
- Pork Rib Porridge *Cháo* 146
- Mushroom Porridge 150
- Crispy Fried Shallots 154
- Chinese Fried 156

RICE VERMICELLI 159
- Vegetable Bún Soup *Bún* 167
- Stir-Fried Beef Bún 172
- Vegan Stir-Fried Bún 174
- Grilled Pork Bún With 176
- Crispy Roasted Pork 180
- Pan-Seared Duck 182

RICE 186
- Butternut Squash 192
- Stir-Fried Beef, ... 194
- Stir-Fried Green 196
- Fried Tofu Braised In 199
- Shrimp In Tangy and 201
- Braised Baby Back 203
- Southern Chicken 205
- Braised Pork and Egg 207
- Braised Chicken in 210
- Braised Mushroom 212
- Salmon In Black 214

DRINKS AND SWEET TREATS 217
- Calamondin / 225
- Sesame Rice 229

Vietnamese Mochi in ... 232
Banana Tapioca ... 235
Mango Tapioca ... 237
Areca Blossom ... 239
Soy Pudding In Ginger ... 241
Crispy Banana ... 243
Panna Cotta With ... 245

Chapter One

THE FLAVORS OF VIETNAM

No matter how badly God wants to punish you, he should not do it when you're eating.

—VIETNAMESE SAYING

Eating is a vital part of life for Vietnamese people. It even shows itself in our casual daily language. The verb ăn, which means "to eat," is present in many action verbs. For example, to dress is to "eat dress" (*ăn mặc*), to speak is to "eat speak" (*ăn nói*), to live is to "eat live" (*ăn ở*), to steal is to "eat steal" (*ăn trộm*). The list goes on. Also, the Vietnamese word for tummy is a metaphor for sincerity—the equivalent of heart in English. From "the bottom of one's heart" would be "from the bottom of one's tummy" in Vietnamese (*từ đáy lòng*); to change one's tummy means to have a change of heart (*thay lòng đổi dạ*); to understand someone's tummy means to understand them very well (*hiểu rõ bụng dạ nhau*); to not have the tummy to do something is to not have the heart to do something (*chẳng còn bụng dạ nào*). Now, can you guess what "kind-hearted" would be in Vietnamese? Yes, it's "kind tummy" (*tốt bụng*)! So don't worry if Vietnamese people comment on your tummy, and be proud if they say you have a good one!

Long story short: We take eating seriously, from the bottom of our tummy. Eating is time-honored and robust in our lexicon, on our streets, and, as you'll soon discover for yourself, in our kitchens.

REGIONAL TASTES

When I was seven years old, my grandparents moved from northern to southern Vietnam to help my uncle start a cashew farm. I didn't see them again until three years later, when my mother and I boarded a southbound train that took three days and two nights to cross the country. I spent most of my time looking out the train's wire-mesh window, feeling as if I was moving from one fairy kingdom to another. The trees, the soil, the sand, and the sea changed their colors as the train brought us farther south. It started with the familiar and endless velvety rice fields and green mountains in the northern provinces. Then came yellow deserted land, marble and rock mountains, emerald sea, and red soil in the central provinces. When we began to see far-stretching orchards where tree branches were low, heavy, and bright with chubby red rambutan and dragon fruits, my mom told me that we had almost reached our final southern stop.

I later learned that the diverse geography (and consequently, climate and culture) I had seen on that train ride accounts for the differences in the taste and seasoning of each region's food. The North, the oldest inhabited area, with its fertile land and strategic geography protected by many big rivers and mountain ranges, has been home to numerous Vietnamese capital cities. Hanoi, the current capital, is more than a thousand years old. The city's longheld proximity to the ruling elites influenced northern cuisine's tendency toward an elegant and refined taste. Typical examples of northern food include the clean but sophisticated phở (noodle soup) and bánh cuốn (steamed rice crêpes). For many people, myself included, these two dishes are favorites for breakfast, lunch, dinner, and even late-night snacks.

Regional Foods of Vietnam

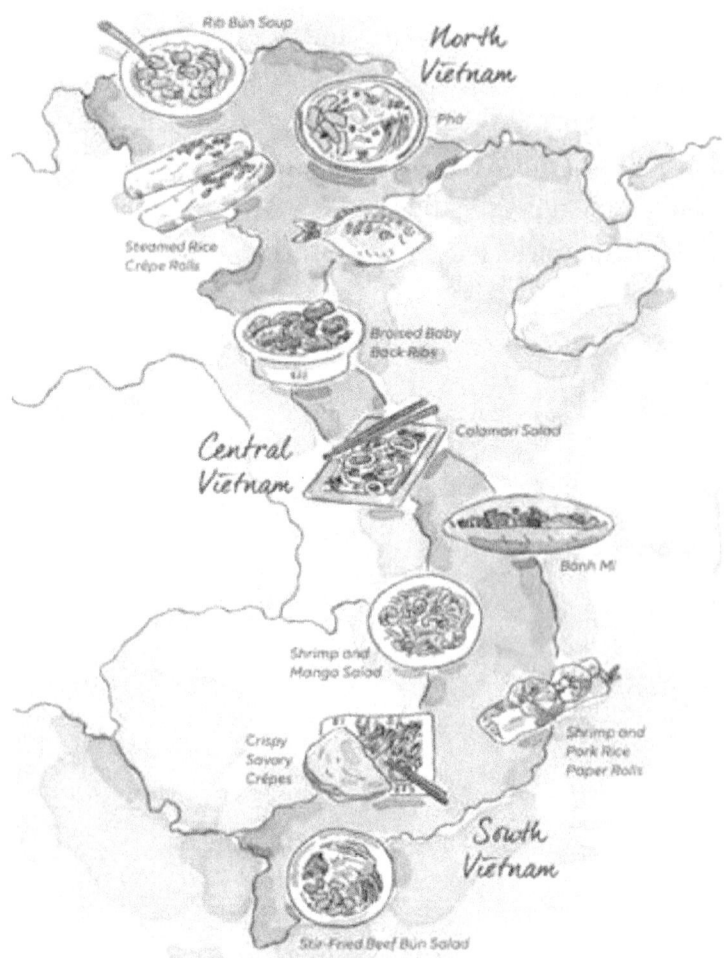

By contrast, the central region of Vietnam is known for food that is so spicy, we say it can tear off your tongue. In ancient times, this region was part of the Indochinese Champa Kingdom that had a strong connection to the Indian subcontinent, hence the spiciness reminiscent of typical Indian food. The people in this region known for its long coastline are fishermen who rely on the sea for a living. Traditional Vietnamese feng shui wisdom says that these people must eat hot or spicy food to keep their body warm against sea water and wind, thereby balancing complementary "yin" and "yang" energies. Both theories make sense to me. When my husband and I first relocated here, we were not used to the heat of this region's food. Anybody watching us eat in a restaurant would have thought we were having a breakup meal—the chili made us cough and sweat profusely.

Southern Vietnam, known for its multicultural blend of Vietnamese, Khmer, Cham, and Chinese influences, is blessed with beautiful tropical weather all year round and fertile land fortified by the Mekong River. This region features its tropical fruits like coconut, tamarind, and pineapple in cooking, and the food here tends to be on the sweeter side compared to the other two regions. Southern chè (Vietnamese-style pudding) and premium quality fruits are well loved throughout our entire country.

ESSENTIAL COMPONENTS OF VIETNAMESE DISHES

Vietnam is a country of 90 million people and 54 ethnic groups, so naturally there are vast differences in eating habits and local produce that I'm not able to fully cover within the scope of this book. However, foods in all three regions are consistent in many aspects because of Vietnam's water rice farming tradition. No matter where one lives in Vietnam, cuisine always contains the essential components of rice, vegetables and herbs, fish sauce, and a harmony between flavors and medicinal properties.

Rice is so important to the Vietnamese that it is synonymous with the word "meal." In social interaction, instead of "How are you?" we greet our friends and acquaintances by saying "Did you eat rice yet?" In the Vietnamese kitchen, steamed rice (cơm) is the most popular variety, eaten every day at home, but there are also rice-based noodles (phở and bún) and rice starch dishes (bánh), usually enjoyed out on the street. And Vietnamese rice culture is so rich that the many names given to it depend on the growing stage of the plant, whether it has husks, whether it's cooked or uncooked, and many other factors.

Fresh turmeric, short bananas (bananitos), and pandan leaves in a vegetable stall in the market.

But a meal can't be made from rice alone. An old Vietnamese idiom goes, "A meal without vegetables is like a disease without cure." It wouldn't be a Vietnamese meal without vegetables and fresh herbs. In fact, to the Vietnamese, vegetables and herbs are one and the same—we call herbs "fragrant vegetables." Since vegetables are a main part of our meal, Vietnamese people for generations have placed great emphasis on seasonal eating to make sure we take advantage of the most delicious vegetables available. I remember my mom scolding my dad for buying water spinach, a summer vegetable, in the fall.

Traditionally, pork and chicken were reserved for big celebrations. Our main source of protein came from the water, with fish being the most popular option. Besides rice and vegetables, a Vietnamese meal included fish, shrimp, and crabs, depending on the availability and season. That has changed now that chicken, pork, and beef are more available, but rice is still essential and vegetables remain a priority.

Another vital component of Vietnamese food is mắm. Mắm is fermented preserved anchovy, shrimp, or crab, which in its original state looks like a paste. Of the many different varieties of mắm, the most popular is nước mắm or fish sauce. *Nước mắm* means "liquid mắm" because it has been filtered to produce a pure liquid. We use it as a dipping sauce or salad dressing, and to add depth and umami (savory) flavor to many dishes. Older folks say a typical Vietnamese meal is truly a gift from nature, with rice and vegetables sourced from our precious soil, and fish and shrimp from our generous waters.

Drive-thru, Vietnamese-style. A family pulls up to a street vendor to pick up a bite to eat. This scooter holds an entire family of four, including a baby sitting on a stool in the front.

STREET FOOD CULTURE

Another important type of Vietnamese food, one that is more internationally known and that makes us very proud, is our street food. Unlike places in the world where street food is associated with simple fast food, Vietnam's street food often includes complex traditional dishes such as different kinds of noodle soups or snacks and desserts made from rice flour. Up until the late 1990s, Vietnamese street food was considered too labor-intensive, complicated, and expensive to make at home. The base ingredient for many of these dishes is freshly ground flour made from rice soaked in water overnight. Today this is easy to make by machine, but it used to be much harder when people had to mill the rice by hand. I know how difficult it was because my grandparents had to grind flour with a heavy stone mill. It took them more than half a day just to prepare the flour. Broth for noodle soup seemingly took forever as well, since people used wood fires that required someone to tend the flame for hours. I know this firsthand as I cooked with wood and dry leaves for five years before switching to coal (see [Life in the Vietnamese Countryside](#)).

    Because of all that time and effort, street food has always been a special treat. Price was also an issue; although it was not expensive, people generally had little money. Vietnamese language has a term for eating street food: *ăn quà*, which literally means "eat presents." Indeed, street food was once considered a fancy present. Phở and chicken porridge were considered special food that only sick people got to eat. When I was small, I would sometimes pretend to be sick so my mom would buy me phở.

    Much has changed in recent years, and street food has become more affordable. People can eat it from early morning to late into the night, for main meals or snacks. Modern restaurants offer a greater selection, but when it comes to traditional noodle soup and bánh, most still opt for street vendors who have been cooking a single dish to perfection every day of their lives, and whose families have been doing so for generations.

    Food vendors, especially those who sell their products in the early morning, carry two baskets on a bamboo rod balanced across their shoulders. Ingredients—and sometimes even the whole stove and pot—are in one basket, while stools, bowls, and chopsticks are in the other. Some vendors still walk around like they did in the old days when vehicles were rare, but usually they go to their usual spot on a sidewalk or street corner. They often start selling as early as 5:00 a.m. because Vietnamese people have the habit of eating breakfast on the street. Diners might sit on tiny stools around a street vendor, those two big bamboo baskets, and a steaming pot. Their food is either in their hand or on a "table," usually another stool. Vendors who sell food on the sidewalk in front of their house often set up communal tables, but space is still limited, especially at popular places. It's common to see people sitting close to each other as if they were couples, or sharing a table as if they were friends, but more often than not they're strangers. We Vietnamese like that—not necessarily the squeezing in and sitting so close to someone, but rather the lively atmosphere of enjoying our food while others enjoy theirs alongside us.

While a street vendor in Vietnam usually sells one specific kind of food, in America, and overseas in general, Vietnamese street food dishes tend to be part of a bigger menu in restaurants. Though these dishes sometimes taste authentic, many people I know, including myself when I lived in New York City, choose to cook traditional street food dishes at home. With the aid of modern kitchen equipment, the cooking process is not as time-intensive as in Vietnam. To illustrate, several years ago in Vietnam I watched my uncle make a dish using a really heavy stone mortar and pestle. I asked him how long the mixture should be pounded. He explained, "Pound it constantly until your arms fall off five times." In America, you can just hit a button and let the food processor do the work for you.

Another reason we cook our street food at home while living overseas is that we can have it whenever we crave it. In Vietnam, a bowl of phở is just a few steps away, be it 5:00 a.m. or midnight. When I was in New York, a bowl of phở or bún would involve a 45-minute train ride, two transfers, and a 15-minute walk, along with the fact that I had to wait until lunchtime to satisfy my breakfast craving.

VIETNAMESE FOOD PHILOSOPHIES

Be it in home cooking or street food, the traditional Vietnamese approach is that ingredients must complement each other to create a balance between yin (cold) and yang (hot). When selecting an ingredient, we look for spices that complement it, thereby keeping the harmony. The result of that harmony is a healthy and delicious dish. Younger generations do not really know much about this theory, but we can still make the right decisions when combining ingredients and spices because knowledge of complementary pairs has been passed down to us by our parents and grandparents. For example, seafood belongs to the cold (yin) group, so we usually eat it with ginger, which is considered hot (yang). Scientifically, seafood is very rich in protein, which might be difficult to digest, so we need ginger, which aids digestion. Plus, according to Vietnamese folklore, ginger also helps those with mild seafood allergies tolerate it better.

Vietnamese harmony also applies to flavors and nutritional content, and is reflected in the different ingredients in a dish and the different dishes in a meal. For example, a meal should balance carbohydrates, water, fiber, protein, and fat. In terms of flavors, a meal is usually a combination of sweet, sour, spicy and salty. This may sound complicated, but in fact this combination can be found in very simple dishes. For example, a bowl of phở provides all five nutritional values: carbohydrates from rice noodles, water from broth, fiber from herbs and onions, protein from meat, and fat from bone marrow. A simple dipping sauce is also a harmony of fish sauce, sugar, lime juice or vinegar, chiles, and garlic—a delightful combination that can make plain steamed vegetables a lot more flavorful.

Vietnamese food is also about flexibility. You might notice that in Vietnamese restaurants, you are offered fish sauce, chiles, lime wedges, and a plate of mixed herbs so you're free to spice your dish to your personal taste. If your broth needs more salt, add some fish sauce; if it's too salty, add some lime. Chiles and mixed herbs are all your choice, and of course you can skip an option if you don't fancy it. Similarly, in a home-cooked meal, soup, rice, meat, and vegetables are served with a bowl of fish sauce in the center so you have the freedom to eat and combine however you like.

VIETNAMESE PANTRY

When I was living with my grandparents in the northern countryside, my grandmother had a spice shop or, to be exact, two bamboo baskets of spices to sell in the market. In the course of preparing her spices for market, she started teaching me about spices when I was very small. My pantry now has more items than my grandmother's, but the spices are basically the same as those stored in our kitchen more than 20 years ago.

Also essential to Vietnamese cuisine are soft-leaf herbs, and the requirement that we include many kinds of raw herbs with every meal makes our cuisine unique. Herbs not only enhance the flavors of other ingredients and boost the aroma of the whole dish, but also contain valuable medicinal properties. A big plate of mixed herbs is a standard part of many dishes, especially those containing bún (rice vermicelli), bánh (rice-based sweet treats), and cuốn (rolls). We also like to add chopped herbs to soup and salads before serving. Herbs are believed to aid digestion and provide medical benefits related to their effect on yin and yang, or the coldness and hotness of a meal, by counteracting extremes for optimum health.

All the herbs, spices, dried foods, and condiments in the following section are available in Asian grocery stores. Some common herbs like cilantro, mint, and dill are available in all supermarkets. Specialty spices are also available on Amazon.

Soft-Leaf Herbs

BASIL With its trademark purple stems, Vietnamese basil is the same as Thai or Asian basil. Basil is one of the most important herbs in Vietnamese cooking, often used in salads and as part of a mixed herb plate. You can substitute the more familiar Italian basil.

CILANTRO Cilantro contributes a flavor that most westerners will recognize from Mexican dishes like salsa. Cilantro is used in Vietnamese cooking in much the same way to provide a pleasant herbal, piquant taste for dishes or herb plates.

DILL Dill is another popular herb in the West, and it pairs well with fish in Vietnamese cooking just as in Western cooking.

Top row, left to right: Shiso leaves; rice paddy herb; saw-tooth/saw-leaf herb. Bottom row, left to right: Vietnamese balm; Vietnamese coriander; lemongrass.

MINT Mint is often served on a big plate of washed herbs to be added to bites of many different types of dishes, or rolled into a wrap with meat and rice vermicelli.

PERILLA LEAF (SHISO) This fragrant herb related to the mint family has a sharp but pleasant flavor. It's usually part of a mixed herb plate. It also pairs well with fish and is added to porridge to treat a cold.

RICE PADDY HERB (NGO OM) This herb is often included in a mixed herb plate, and is also used in seafood soup. It provides a spicy taste that is a bit like cumin and complements many types of dishes.

SAW-TOOTH/SAW-LEAF HERB Also known as culantro (not a typo!), it is, as one of its names suggests, a saw-toothed herb with long leaves that has a strong but pleasant taste. We often break it into pieces as we add it to noodle soups.

VIETNAMESE BALM This herb smells like a combination of lemon and mint. It's usually added to salads and mixed herb plates. It pairs very well with crispy fried tofu.

VIETNAMESE CORIANDER (RAU RĂM) This is also known as Vietnamese mint. Confusing, I know, but both names work when you do a web search on this herb. It has a peppery flavor and is often served with poultry dishes.

Hard Herbs and Roots

GINGER Ginger is a great accompaniment to poultry, fish, and beef. I also use ginger juice mixed with salt water to wash duck and fish to get rid of any unpleasant smell. Charred ginger and shallot are nice to have in broth because of their lovely aroma.

LEMONGRASS Lemongrass has a wonderful therapeutic aroma (it is often used in Vietnamese spas), plus it aids digestion. We use it for tea, in broth, and to marinate meat. The stalk of lemongrass has to be bruised to release the oil before using. A meat hammer is useful for bruising lemongrass stalks.

SHALLOTS Shallots are a must-have in a Vietnamese pantry. They're an important ingredient in many stir-fry dishes and soups, and in marinades for meat and fish. I also make [Crispy Fried Shallots](#) for salads, porridge, omelets, and fried rice toppings.

GARLIC Along with shallots, garlic is another Vietnamese pantry staple. Garlic is important in not only marinades, stir-fries, and braised dishes, but also in the signature sweet and sour salad dressing and dipping sauce.

Keeping Herbs Fresh

Most Vietnamese herbs are soft-leaf, which are much more difficult to preserve than hardier herbs like rosemary and thyme. To keep them fresh in the refrigerator, it's important to make sure that they're dry and in an airtight container. I usually pick off the dead leaves and stems, wrap the remainder in paper towels, and seal them in an airtight zip-top bag. Sometimes I divide them into small individual portions and keep them in separate bags. I keep herbs in the bottom of the refrigerator, where they usually last for a week.

Spices

FIVE-SPICE POWDER The Chinese introduced this powder to Vietnam long ago. It contains cardamom, star anise, cloves, cumin, and cinnamon. I use this complex spice in roasted pork, duck, and beef stews.

TURMERIC Vietnamese cooks use turmeric in fish dishes to enhance the color of the fish and eliminate the fishy smell. We also use it for natural food coloring. Turmeric has great skin-healing properties, so many women eat dishes with turmeric after giving birth. When an open wound starts to heal, we apply fresh turmeric juice on it to prevent scars. Although I have turmeric in both fresh and powder forms, I find turmeric powder easier to manage since fresh turmeric usually turns my spoon, cutting board, knife, and nails yellow.

BLACK CARDAMOM SEEDS This is one of the key spices in classic beef phở stock. Vietnamese cuisine uses black cardamom in whole seed form as opposed to ground cardamom, which is more common in Western baking. Black cardamom seeds are usually dry-roasted in a pan before being added to beef phở stock.

STAR ANISE These dry flowers are another important spice in beef phở stock. They also need to be dry-roasted to release fragrance before cooking.

CINNAMON BARK/STICKS This is the third essential spice in the beef phở spice trio. Just like the other two, cinnamon sticks should be dry-roasted in a pan to release their wonderful aroma before adding to the stock. You can buy black cardamom seeds, star anise, and cinnamon sticks separately or packaged together in a phở spice mix.

Condiments

FISH SAUCE (NUOC MAM) Fish sauce is Vietnam's ubiquitous condiment, used to season salad dressing and dipping sauce, to marinate meat, and to add to soup and many other dishes right before serving to create a rich umami flavor. Nước mắm has gradations of quality and flavor as complex as any wine or olive oil. Make sure you choose a bottle made with anchovy (cá cơm) and salt only, as some lower-quality versions include unnecessary or unhealthy additional ingredients. Learn more in Fish Sauces and Pastes.

Top row, left to right: Fish sauce; rice vinegar; soy sauce. Bottom row, left to right: Tamarind fruit; dried rice vermicelli noodles; coconut milk.

HONEY I often brush honey on barbecued meat to create a delicious golden glaze, or just dip a fresh bánh mì baguette (see <u>here</u>) into it when I have a craving!

RICE VINEGAR I use rice vinegar interchangeably with freshly squeezed lime juice in the signature Vietnamese sweet and sour sauce for rolls, salads, and some cold noodle dishes. It has a milder taste compared to other kinds of vinegar and a lower acidity than Western grape- or wine-derived vinegars.

SOY SAUCE I like to use soy sauce to marinate thinly sliced beef before stir-frying, as a dipping sauce for vegan dishes, with peanut sauce for fresh spring rolls, and as a condiment in braised vegan dishes. There are tremendous differences in quality; for more details, see <u>Soy Sauces: Not All Created Equal.</u>

TAMARIND PASTE/PULP I use tamarind paste to add a nice sourness to my southern-inspired <u>Sweet and Sour Fish Soup</u>. I also mix it in southern-style dipping sauces and glazes. Before using, the paste has to be soaked in hot water for about 15 minutes. Then you can use your hand to break it apart and strain the mixture. Make sure to discard seeds, if any. Prepared pastes are also available at many Asian markets.

Soy Sauces: Not All are Created Equal

The most famous soy sauce in Vietnam is Bần soy sauce or tương Bần, named after a small rural town in the north of Vietnam. Bần soy sauce is so delicious and well known that it was once a specialty offered to kings. This soy sauce has a honey color, a pleasant aroma, and a complex flavor with a sweet finish. It's made in a time-intensive process using premium-quality soy beans, the best glutinous rice, and salt, combined and then fermented in carefully selected ceramic pots.

How do I know so much about Bần soy sauce? Well, Bần happens to be my hometown, and my father's family has had a tradition of making soy sauce for many generations. I knew those beautiful soy fields like the back of my hand, and I used to love helping my grandparents make soy sauce, which we would package in cans and sell on the road in front of my house.

As you might imagine, I can be pretty picky when it comes to soy sauce. When I was in the US, I couldn't find any soy sauce of the Bần standard of quality, but I was reasonably happy with Kikkoman's naturally brewed soy sauce. The texture is different from Vietnamese soy sauce because it has been filtered, but the flavor is harmonious with the Vietnamese dishes that I've paired it with. Regular Kikkoman soy sauce has wheat in it, so if you're gluten-free, make sure to opt for their gluten-free version.

Top row, left to right: Dried shiitake mushrooms; glass noodles; rice flour. Bottom row, left to right: Rice papers; tapioca pearls; tapioca starch.

Other Essentials

COCONUT MILK I use canned coconut milk in curry and in Vietnamese pudding desserts to add a creamy texture. My go-to brand is Aroy-D.

DRIED MUSHROOMS (WOOD EAR OR SHIITAKE) I use these mushrooms as filling in fried rolls ([Nem Rán](#)) and steamed crêpes ([Bánh Cuốn](#)). They have a crunchy texture and earthy flavor. Before cooking, soak the dried mushrooms in hot water for 15 minutes, then wash and squeeze them to remove excess water.

DRIED PHO AND RICE VERMICELLI NOODLES In Vietnam, I buy fresh noodles in the market, but dried noodles are usually the only kind available outside Asia. But I'm happy to share with you my trick to making dried noodles taste exactly like fresh ones. First, soak the dried noodles in a bowl of cool water for 30 to 40 minutes. In a large pot, bring a generous amount of water to a boil over medium-high heat. Transfer the noodles to the boiling water and cook for 5 minutes, stirring occasionally. Drain and immediately rinse the noodles under running water to cool. Drain again for 10 to 15 minutes to let the noodles dry out a bit before serving. You can keep boiled noodles in the refrigerator for a week. Before serving, boil the noodles again for 5 minutes and repeat the draining process.

GLASS NOODLES These transparent noodles are made from mung bean starch or canna starch. They're used in noodle soup, usually with chicken, and in this book I use them in fried roll fillings ([chapter 2](#)).

OIL I use oil for stir-frying, pan-frying, and deep-frying. Any mild oil will do, such as canola, peanut, sunflower seed, or light sesame oil (not toasted sesame oil, which is used for seasoning rather than cooking).

RICE I eat steamed rice almost every day with meat and vegetable dishes like those you'll see in [chapter 8](#). I often buy jasmine or sushi rice.

RICE FLOUR AND GLUTINOUS RICE FLOUR I use these products to make traditional Vietnamese [bánh](#). Rice flour provides a crunchy texture, while glutinous or sticky rice flour gives a chewy texture. It's common to mix these two flours together. For certain bánh dishes like [Bánh Xèo](#) and [Bánh Cuốn](#), I use premixed packages for convenience and certainty that I'm getting the ratios right.

RICE PAPERS I use round rice paper sheets for making all kinds of fried and fresh roll dishes. There are several different sizes, but I recommend the ones that are around 8 inches in diameter. Smaller ones are slightly more difficult to fold and roll, but they can still work well with a bit of extra patience and practice. To roll, I quickly soak each rice paper sheet in a big bowl of lukewarm water so that it gets soft before using. After a bit of practice, you'll find just the right length of time to soak for the perfect wrapper!

TAPIOCA PEARLS Not to be confused with tapioca starch, tapioca pearls are an essential part of Vietnamese desserts and Southeast Asian desserts in general.

TAPIOCA STARCH Tapioca starch is a common thickening agent in Vietnamese cooking, especially common in our pudding.

Life in the Vietnamese Countryside

When I was growing up in the late 1980s, we had electricity only at certain hours of the day. We usually didn't have electricity at night, so we used oil lamps for lighting. In summer months it was the opposite. Power outages occurred from very early morning until past midnight, largely because power demand would rise dramatically due to the heat. Basically, we had just a few hours of electricity every day. We used to eat dinner on a mat in our front yard because it was too hot and dark inside.

Until I was 10 years old, my family cooked with dry leaves, rice husks, straw, and wood. It was very common for people in the countryside to cook with these materials. It's like a campfire, but inside the kitchen. The traditional Vietnamese kitchen was a small shed, built as a separate structure a few meters away from the house in order to keep the heat and smoke away from the living areas. Gas stoves didn't exist back then. Even dry wood was not always available. (My mother had to wait in line for hours to buy wood!) More affluent families in the city cooked with tiny kerosene stoves. In the mid-1990s, coal was more widely available, so many families switched to a coal stove.

 My family got a gas stove sometime around 2001, but we rarely used it and still relied on our coal stove. Gas was expensive, so we used the gas stove only when we were too busy and didn't have time to start the fire on the coal stove. Even today, many houses in the Vietnamese countryside still use wood stoves.

 Despite our limited resources, we were able to make delicious food — even enough to share with those around us. Imagine what easy, tasty Vietnamese food you will make with all of today's handy tools at your disposal!

COOKING TOOLS

As mentioned earlier, Vietnamese cooking is all about flexibility and simplicity, and this is reflected in the tools we use. Besides basics like a sauté pan or skillet, saucepans, and a stockpot, the following are the most frequently used equipment and utensils in a Vietnamese kitchen.

CHOPSTICKS The most ubiquitous utensil in any Vietnamese cook's kitchen is the humble chopstick. We are able to use chopsticks for so many cooking tasks you'd be amazed. Vietnamese use these simple sticks to pick, to flip, to stir, and to serve food. This is true whether they're used in a boiling pot, over a hot grill, or in a sauté pan.

FINE-MESH SKIMMER You can use a spoon, but a small fine-mesh skimmer works best to skim the foam off the top of your pot when making beef or chicken stock.

HEAVY MORTAR AND PESTLE A heavy mortar and pestle set, made of wood, stone, or granite, is essential for prepping your aromatics. Pounding garlic, shallot, and ginger allows you to release their fragrance far better than does chopping. Because it is difficult and expensive to get a stand mixer or grinder in Vietnam, I also use my mortar and pestle to pound ground meat into a fine, consistent paste when making sausage.

KITCHEN SCISSORS Many Vietnamese, and indeed many Asians, like to use scissors to cut cooked food. It might sound strange, but once you see what a perfect tool scissors can be for cutting food, you'll be converted, too. When your food is chewy and super-hot, cutting with a knife can be a big challenge. Try scissors to cut fried rolls, crêpes, and hot tofu when they are sizzling, fresh out of the pan.

RICE COOKER If you like rice but can't seem to get the consistency right, I highly recommend purchasing a rice cooker. A basic model costs only around $20 and will save you a lot of time. More importantly, it creates a perfect bowl of rice every time, unlike the stove top method, which can be challenging to get right. Many westerners are surprised to find out that a rice cooker works really well for other cooking tasks like cooking beans and porridge or making hotpot (an Asian fondue) for a table of hungry friends.

TEA BALL This is a handy tool when you make phở. Putting spices in a tea ball makes it convenient to remove them from the pot without having to fish around in the hot broth with a spoon or sieve.

Top row, left to right: Chopsticks; fine-mesh skimmer; heavy mortar and pestle. Bottom row, left to right: Kitchen scissors; rice cooker; tea ball.

COOKING TECHNIQUES

Vietnamese traditional cooking techniques tend to focus on skills that can be used under the most common kitchen conditions: cooking over open fire in a pan or pot without relying on gas stoves, microwaves, blenders, or other electrical kitchen appliances. However, in this book we'll take advantage of modern conveniences from time to time, so don't worry!

BOILING Boiling is very common in Vietnamese cooking. We like to boil vegetables and meat to preserve the natural freshness of the food, and we'll use the boiled water afterward to make soup. Nothing goes to waste! Adding a teaspoon of salt to the water raises the boiling point, which helps the food keep its natural colors and enhances the flavors. When boiling vegetables, we bring salt water to a boil first, then add the vegetables. Boiling meat is slightly different. We tend to add meat to cold water with a little salt and then bring it to a boil. Usually we also add some aromatics, like ginger and shallot, when boiling meat.

BLANCHING Blanching is basically the same as boiling, but quicker and with an extra step. We often blanch vegetables before stir-frying. To blanch, we bring salted water to a boil, then immerse the vegetables in the water for up to a minute depending on the kind of vegetables. For example, broccoli and root vegetables take a bit longer than soft-leaf vegetables. Then we transfer the vegetables to a bowl of ice water to halt the cooking process. As soon as the vegetables cool, they are drained. The cold water also helps preserve the bright, fresh color of vegetables and makes them crunchy.

STIR-FRYING Vietnamese cooking includes a lot of stir-frying with vegetables or vegetable-meat combinations. Stir-frying involves frying food rapidly over high heat. Because of the high temperatures and quick cooking times, stirring must be constant. We often add minced shallot or garlic to the frying oil to release their fragrance before adding food. At home, I stir-fry vegetables almost every day as a side dish for lunch or dinner.

SLOW-COOKING Slow-cooking is a very popular technique in Vietnamese cooking, specifically for making bone broth for noodle soups and for braising meat or fish. The length of time varies depending on the kind of meat used. Beef takes the longest time, whereas fish and shellfish cook the fastest. We bring the food to a boil over medium-high heat, then reduce the heat to low and simmer for several minutes to several hours. We often add charred ginger or shallot to slow-cooked bone broth to enhance the flavor. When braising, food can be marinated with caramel sauce, fish or soy sauce, and pepper.

GRILLING Vietnamese cooks traditionally use charcoal in a small clay grill for this cooking method. Many people don't grill at home. We mostly get and eat our grilled food on a sidewalk somewhere, since not every house has a space appropriate for grilling due to smoke and heat concerns. For the best flavor, it's ideal to grill over charcoal, but sometimes in rainy weather or when I'm too hungry to wait, I cook indoors using a grill pan on my stove top and it works very well.

DEEP-FRYING I use a small saucepan for deep-frying to save oil and to keep the heat concentrated. The key to deep-frying is to wait to add the food until the oil is hot enough (about 390°F). You can check with a thermometer. I have a nice infrared one, but I can't always find it when I need it, so I often check the temperature the old-fashioned Vietnamese way—by dipping that handy chopstick into the oil. If the oil sizzles, then it's ready. If you don't have chopsticks, a fork works just as well.

STEAMING There are several steaming methods used in Vietnamese cooking, depending on the kind of food and the desired result. The most common method is to use a steamer or a steaming basket inside a pot of boiling water. This method is good for food that has little fat content and needs hydration to cook, like sticky rice, some types of bánh, and sausage.

Shrimp and Pork Rice Paper Rolls

Chapter Two

Cuốn
ROLLS

Sweet and Sour Fish Sauce Dip *Nước Mắm Chua Ngọt*

Peanut Soy Sauce Dip *Tương Đậu Phông*

Shrimp and Pork Rice Paper Rolls *Gỏi Cuốn*

Vegan Fresh Rolls *Gỏi Cuốn Chay*

Fried Pork and Egg Rolls *Nem Rán*

Vegan Fried Rolls *Chả Giò Chay*

Grilled / Roasted Shrimp Sausage Rolls *Chạo Tôm*

Pan-Seared Beef with Mustard Green Rolls *Bò Cuốn Lá Cải*

Grilled Beef in Wild Betel Leaf Rolls *Bò Cuốn Lá Lốt*

Roasted Fish with Dill, Ginger, and Scallion Rolls *Cá Cuốn*

Cuốn, **pronounced "kuon," means "roll" in Vietnamese.** You might think the name sounds a bit generic, but that's just an indication of how versatile and varied this dish is. Unlike rolls in the West, these dishes involve wrapping and rolling rice paper around different combinations of vegetables, meat, or seafood. One of the most popular versions is to wrap meat and vegetables and pan-fry the roll, serving it crispy and hot just out of the sizzling oil. Another favorite is to wrap cooked meat, vegetables, and herbs and then eat the roll fresh and soft, always with a dipping sauce to give it a bit of kick and contrasting flavor.

The soft, fresh type of cuốn originated in the central and southern regions of Vietnam, which enjoy tropical weather all year round. People there have had influences from various regions in Asia, and they were (and still are) believed to be more casual and easygoing than their northern counterparts. This open nature is reflected in the variety of dishes from that region that require food to be eaten with the hands. The soft cuốn is gaining popularity around the rest of the country because it is easier to make and fun to eat, especially for gatherings, where everyone can customize their own cuốn and add whatever ingredients they want to each roll.

There are two characteristics of cuốn that Vietnamese people are proud of. First, because of the harmony among vegetables, herbs, and protein, cuốn is satisfying but also very light. You can eat until you're satisfied, but you never feel overly full. And second, cuốn is a feast for all five senses. The colors look enticing. The sweet, sour, salty, and spicy flavors taste great, and of course the fresh herbs and seasoned fillings make the aroma alluring. Our ears hear the delightful crunch of vegetables or the crisp of rice paper. And our hands feel the freshness of herbs and other ingredients in this handheld treat.

You'll need a few things to get started. The perfect partner for cuốn dishes is a bowl of good dipping sauce—this is a must, so I've included two sauce recipes in this chapter. Then you need something to wrap and roll, usually rice papers. Rice papers should be briefly soaked in lukewarm water to soften them before rolling. If this dish is part of a family meal, everybody can have a bowl of lukewarm water by their side to roll their own cuốn. And as with most Vietnamese dishes, all ingredients in cuốn are created to taste preferences, which is nice since you don't have to follow a strict formula to cook a great dish. Pick the herbs and vegetables that you like best. Make sure they're seasonal and local. Pick a favorite protein, whether meat, fish, or tofu. Then you're ready to wrap, roll, and awaken your five senses!

Like a timeless piece of clothing in your closet that can be dressed up or down, cuốn can be minimally elegant or beautifully messy. You can make mini rolls for fancy, manageable finger foods. And to make it fun, you can set out the ingredients on the dining table at gatherings and family meals, letting each person pick and roll whatever they like.

Dipping Sauce (NUOc ChAm) at the Center of the Table

Nước means liquid or water, and chấm *means to dip, so nước chấm is sauce for dipping. Along with rice-based food, nước chấm is one of the prime staples at the the center of our meals. The nước chấm that accompanies our daily home meals of vegetables, steamed rice, and fish or tofu, is generally quite simple: just pure fish sauce with some optional minced chile to give it a bit of heat. Nước chấm for cuốn and bánh, however, is more complex, and contains a mix of sweet, sour, salty, and spicy flavors to create balance with the meat, vegetables, herbs, and even the rice paper wrap. Once you know how to make a bowl of nước chấm that's right for your meal, you'll enjoy greater authenticity and flavor!*

The best known nước chấm, both internationally and domestically, is [Sweet and Sour Fish Sauce Dip.](#) It pairs well with all the rolled dishes in this chapter, as well as with many other dishes in the following chapters. Beside this variety of nước chấm, each region has its own special favorites like shrimp paste sauce, peanut sauce, anchovy pineapple sauce, or tamarind sauce.

However, most places in Vietnam offer a basic sweet and sour fish sauce dip in addition to any other local sauce variations because it is the most popular and the most versatile.

Sweet and Sour Fish Sauce Dip *Nước Mắm Chua Ngọt*

SERVES 1 • PREP TIME: 10 MINUTES

"Little Miss Dipping Sauce" was the nickname my uncle gave me. My dad had seven siblings, and we would all gather for lunch on the First of Tết (Vietnamese New Year—akin to Christmas morning in Vietnam). My job was to mix the fish sauce dip and make pickles, and these tasks took me the whole morning. This is my recipe from 15 years of being Little Miss Dipping Sauce for our family feast. I usually make it fresh because it's quick to make, but it can be refrigerated for up to two weeks. If you make it ahead of time, wait to add the minced garlic and chile until just before serving.

1½ tablespoons freshly squeezed lime juice

1 tablespoon cool water

1½ tablespoons sugar

1 tablespoon fish sauce

1 tablespoon minced garlic

1½ teaspoons minced hot chile

In a small bowl, whisk the lime juice, water, and sugar until the sugar dissolves. Add the fish sauce and stir well. Add the minced garlic and chile and serve.

Substitution tip: *You can use rice vinegar in place of the lime juice if you don't have fresh limes on hand.*

Cooking tip: *The foolproof way to make a perfect sweet and sour dipping sauce is to mix a bowl of perfect limeade first. Mix the lime juice, water, and sugar to see if the sweet and sour flavors are balanced. Then gradually add the* *fish sauce, teaspoon by teaspoon, and taste along the way. Make sure to use cool water—this will allow the minced garlic and hot chile to float, creating a bright, colorful sauce. Lukewarm water will make the garlic and hot chile sink to the bottom of the bowl.*

Fish Sauces and Pastes

Depending on the amount of fish and salt involved in a fish sauce's fermentation process, nước mắm varies in protein and sodium content. The higher protein versions, expressed in degrees (35 or 40 degrees being a desirable number), are the most flavorful and expensive to make. All nước mắm varieties are salty, so when making dipping sauce or salad dressing, you can add water to reduce the sauce's saltiness to your desired level.

Many people are concerned about cooking with fish sauce because they've heard that it has a strong smell, but better-quality nước mắm is pure and has quite a pleasant aroma. Other people may have had a reaction after smelling fish sauce directly from the bottle. Even the finest perfume can smell strong and possibly off-putting if you sniff it directly from the bottle, but once the fish sauce is used in a recipe, it enhances rather than overpowers the dish. My all-time favorite brand is Red Boat fish sauce, which is available on Amazon. It uses anchovies from Phú Quốc, a lovely tropical island with white sand beaches. It also brews the most famous fish sauce in Vietnam. This variety has a wonderful aroma and complex flavor that enhances any dish calling for the sauce.

Besides nước mắm, each region has its own versions of mắm, whether it be shrimp paste, anchovy paste, or crab paste. However, these pastes are used less frequently than fish sauce. There's a love-hate relationship with pastes, even among Vietnamese people, because of their very strong smell. We joke that if you really loathe someone, just drop a little shrimp paste in front of their house. Shrimp paste and fine shrimp paste are available on Amazon and in Vietnamese or Asian markets. However, dishes will still be delicious with regular fish sauce, and you're still eating legitimately Vietnamese style if you choose not to use pastes.

Peanut Soy Sauce Dip

Tương Dâu Phông

SERVES 1 • PREP TIME: 10 MINUTES • COOK TIME: 5 MINUTES

Peanut soy sauce is very popular in central and southern Vietnam. Any food dipped into this sauce beneJts from its creamy, nutty, and buttery texture, a nice counterpoint to a savory meat and spicy herb Jlling. The traditional recipe calls for Vietnamese soy sauce (with beans) and sweet rice porridge to thicken it and add a nice rice fragrance, as well as minced pork or pork liver to create a fatty, creamy texture. However, today many people like to substitute peanut butter, which provides a similar texture to pork but is easier to work with. Since it can be challenging to Jnd Vietnamese soy sauce and fresh coconut juice overseas, the following recipe is a modern, simpliJed version that still retains the traditional, authentic flavors and texture.

1 tablespoon soy sauce

1 tablespoon rice vinegar

1 tablespoon sugar

1 tablespoon vegetable oil

1 tablespoon minced garlic

1½ tablespoons peanut butter

1 tablespoon roasted peanuts, chopped

1. In a small bowl, whisk the soy sauce, rice vinegar, and sugar until the sugar dissolves.

2. Heat the oil in a small saucepan over high heat. Add the garlic and stir-fry for about 1 minute, until fragrant and slightly golden. Reduce the heat to low.

3. Add the soy sauce mixture to the saucepan and stir well for about 30 seconds.

4. Add the peanut butter and stir well until the sauce is smooth. Remove from the heat and transfer the dip to a small bowl. Sprinkle with the roasted peanuts before serving.

Cooking tip: *To give the sauce a spicy kick, add minced hot chiles or paprika and stir-fry it with the garlic in step 2.*

Shrimp and Pork Rice Paper Rolls *Gỏi Cuốn*

MAKES 10 ROLLS • SERVES 2 • PREP TIME: 30 MINUTES • COOK TIME: 30 MINUTES

Gỏi means salad in the central and southern regions of Vietnam, and cuốn means rolls. So the name of this southern dish means salad rolls. Overseas they're better known as fresh rolls to distinguish them from fried rolls. This particular roll is traditionally served with peanut sauce; however, many places in Vietnam also serve it with sweet and sour fish sauce. Sweet and sour fish sauce gives it an elegant taste, while peanut sauce offers a bold, creamy texture.

The vegetables and herbs below are just suggestions. You can simply use one kind of herb and one kind of vegetable if you like. Sometimes I'm too hungry to prepare anything complicated and will use only three ingredients: vermicelli, shrimp, and mint — and they are still absolutely delicious.

1 shallot, lightly smashed (optional)

1 teaspoon salt

4 ounces pork loin, shoulder, or belly

15 jumbo shrimp, peeled and deveined

1 (2-inch) piece ginger, lightly smashed (optional)

½ cup fresh mint leaves

½ cup fresh basil leaves

½ cup fresh cilantro leaves

10 (8-inch) rice paper sheets

1 head lettuce (preferably butterhead/butter lettuce because their smaller leaves fit better in a roll)

4 ounces rice vermicelli, cooked according to package instructions (or see here)

1 cucumber (preferably English), shredded

10 garlic chives, cut into 3-inch strips (optional)

2 recipes Sweet and Sour Fish Sauce Dip or Peanut Soy Sauce Dip

To cook the pork

1. Put 1 cup water in a saucepan.
2. Add the shallot (if using) and salt. Stir until the salt dissolves, then bring to a boil over high heat. Add the pork, cover, and reduce the heat to medium. The water should cover the pork.
3. Cook for about 20 minutes, depending on the thickness of the pork. Check for doneness by piercing a fork or a chopstick all the way through the meat. If the juice runs clear, it's done. If the juice is pink, continue cooking another few minutes.
4. Transfer the pork to a bowl of ice water or rinse under running water until completely cool. Drain well and cut into thin slices. Set aside.

To cook the shrimp

1. While the pork is cooking, wash the shrimp and leave damp. Put the shrimp in another saucepan, along with the ginger (if using).
2. Cover and cook over medium heat, stirring once, until the shrimp is pink and opaque, about 7 minutes.
3. Transfer the shrimp to a bowl of ice water until cool. Drain well and halve the shrimp lengthwise for easier rolling.

To assemble the rolls

1. Combine the mint, basil, and cilantro in a small bowl.
2. Fill a large bowl with lukewarm water and prepare a flat, dry surface, like a platter or cutting board that is larger than the rice papers.
3. Dip a sheet of rice paper into the water. Soak it so it becomes soft but not limp, then remove the paper and gently shake off the excess water. The paper

should be flexible enough to fold without cracking. Stretch the paper on the flat surface.

4. Place a lettuce leaf and a scoop each of the vermicelli, mint, basil, and cilantro, and cucumber onto the edge of the paper nearest to you, leaving 1 inch uncovered at the edge and on both sides. Add 1 or 2 slices of pork and 3 slices of shrimp. Keep the pink side of the shrimp down.

5. Start rolling from the edge nearest to you toward the center of the rice paper, folding the edges on both sides toward the center.

6. Add 2 or 3 garlic chive pieces (if using), leaving 1 inch of the stems showing outside the roll for presentation, and finish rolling it up.

7. Repeat with the remaining rolls. Serve with your choice of dipping sauce.

Substitution tip: If you like mangos and they're in season, you can replace the cucumber with mango. It pairs well with shrimp and makes a natural sweet and sour combination.

Cooking tip: If you're wondering why halving the shrimp is recommended, thick shrimp might break the rice paper and also makes the roll look bumpy. That said, rolling the whole shrimp is absolutely fine.

Vegan Fresh Rolls *Gỏi Cuốn Ch*

SERVES 2 (4 ROLLS EACH) • PREP TIME: 30 MINUTES • COOK TIME: 20 MINUTES

Gỏi cuốn chay is served in many vegetarian restaurants in the central and southern regions, and you don't have to be vegan to love it. Even if you think you don't like tofu, please give this a try. Crispy fried tofu is really delicious, like a cheese stick. I feel certain it'll convert you.

You get an A for authenticity if you can Jnd Vietnamese balm leaves (rau kinh giới), tofu's best friend. I originally thought balm leaves were rare in the United States, but I've found them at Vietnamese grocers in New York's Chinatown. I also discovered that my Swedish-American mother-in-law planted them in her garden in Seattle. She didn't know what they were, but liked their pleasant minty fragrance. Imagine my surprise and delight!

1 (10-ounce) block firm tofu

¼ cup vegetable oil

1½ tablespoons soy sauce

½ cup fresh mint leaves

½ cup fresh cilantro leaves

½ cup Vietnamese balm leaves (optional)

1 head small-leafed lettuce (preferably butterhead or butter lettuce)

3 ounces rice vermicelli, cooked according to package instructions (or see here)

1 cucumber (preferably English), shredded

8 (8-inch) rice paper sheets

2 recipes Peanut Soy Sauce Dip

To fry the tofu

1. Pat the tofu dry with a paper towel, the drier, the better to reduce spattering when frying. Halve the tofu lengthwise and then cut it crosswise into 8 pieces.
2. Heat a medium sauté pan over medium-high heat. Swirl in the oil to spread it evenly. Add the tofu, flat-side down, and fry until golden on the bottom, about 7 minutes. Flip and fry the other side until golden, about 5 minutes.
3. Transfer the tofu to a large bowl. While the tofu is still hot, drizzle the soy sauce over the tofu and gently toss. When the tofu cools, halve each piece lengthwise using a knife or scissors for easier rolling, if desired.

To assemble the rolls

1. Combine the mint, cilantro, and balm leaves in a small bowl.
2. Fill a large bowl with lukewarm water and prepare a flat, dry surface, like a platter or cutting board that is larger than the rice papers.
3. Dip a sheet of rice paper into the bowl. Soak it so it becomes soft but not limp, then remove the paper and gently shake off the excess water. The paper should be flexible enough to fold without cracking. Stretch the paper on the flat surface.
4. Place a lettuce leaf and a scoop each of the vermicelli, mint, cilantro, and balm leaves, and cucumber at the edge of the paper nearest to you, leaving 1 inch on that edge and on both sides. Add 4 pieces of tofu. Start rolling from the edge nearest to you toward the center of the rice paper, folding the excess on both sides in toward the center. Roll the paper the rest of the way until tight and even.
5. Repeat with the remaining rolls. Serve with the dipping sauce.

> ***Substitution tip:** Instead of cucumber, you can use Carrot and Daikon Pickles to add a sweet and sour essence.*
>
> ***Cooking tip:** Be sure to stand back when the tofu is frying—it tends to spatter a bit!*

Fried Pork and Egg Rolls   m Rán

MAKES 15 ROLLS • PREP TIME: 45 MINUTES • COOK TIME: 20 MINUTES

Nem rán is one of my all-time favorites. In the North, we simply call it nem. When I think of nem, I think of our festive season, the Vietnamese New Year feast, and the aroma of agarwood incense. I remember my tiny mother chopping meat and rolling nem on the dirt floor of our narrow kitchen in the chilly winter, the two of us huddled next to the tiny coal oven for warmth. My mom did the rolling and I did the frying. We used coal or wood ovens. It was difficult to control the flame and the food would burn easily unless I kept a watchful eye on it. My mom always rolled a few tiny nem for my little brother and me. Since we had nem only once a year, the crispy, delicious golden mini nem fresh off the sizzling pan was like a Christmas present to us. The following is my mother's recipe and is a treat for lunch or dinner.

- 1 ounce dried shiitake or wood ear mushrooms (optional)
- 1 ounce glass noodles (optional)
- 1 pound ground pork
- 5 large eggs, lightly beaten
- 1 cup shredded carrot
- 2 tablespoons minced shallot
- ¼ teaspoon salt
- 1 teaspoon freshly ground black pepper
- 15 (8-inch) rice paper sheets
- Vegetable oil, for frying
- 3 recipes Sweet and Sour Fish Sauce Dip
- 2 cups fresh herbs, such as cilantro, mint, and basil (optional)

To prepare the filling

1. Soak the dried mushrooms (if using) in boiling water for 15 minutes. Drain and squeeze out the excess water. Trim off the hard ends if using wood ear mushrooms, then shred and chop. Set aside.
2. Soak the glass noodles (if using) in water for 15 minutes. Drain and cut the noodles into 1-inch pieces, then set aside.
3. In a large bowl, combine the pork, eggs, carrot, mushrooms, noodles, shallot, salt, and pepper, and mix well.

To assemble the rolls

1. Fill a large bowl with lukewarm water and prepare a flat, dry surface, like a platter or cutting board that is larger than the rice papers.
2. Dip a sheet of rice paper into the bowl. Soak it so it becomes soft but not limp, then remove the paper and gently shake off the excess water. The paper should be flexible enough to fold without cracking. Stretch the rice paper on the flat surface.
3. Place a spoonful of the pork mixture on the rice paper. Using your fingers, shape the mixture into a cylinder that stretches toward the sides of the paper.
4. Start rolling from the edge nearest to you toward the center of the rice paper, folding the excess on both sides in toward the center. Roll the paper the rest of the way until tight and even.
5. Repeat with the remaining rolls, leaving space between them to avoid sticking.

To fry the rolls

1. In a medium nonstick sauté pan, pour in the oil to a depth of ¼ inch and heat over high heat until it reaches about 390°F. Check with a thermometer or by dipping a chopstick into the oil. If the oil sizzles, it's ready. You can also check by lowering a roll into the oil.
2. Reduce the heat to medium and add the rolls, giving them space. Fry until one side is golden. Flip and fry until the other side is golden.

3. Transfer the rolls to paper towels to drain.

4. Serve immediately with the dipping sauce and herbs, if desired. You can either eat the rolls whole or use a pair of scissors to cut them into 3 or 4 bite-size pieces.

> **Substitution tip:** Instead of pork, you can make nem with ground chicken, ground beef, or crabmeat.
>
> **Variation tip:** You can cut these fried rolls into bite-size pieces and arrange them in a noodle salad bowl with rice vermicelli (bún, cooked per the package instructions) and herbs like mint, cilantro, and basil. Pour the sweet and sour fish sauce over, stir to mix, and serve.
>
> **Cooking tip:** You can fry these rolls up to 4 hours in advance, then reheat them in a hot sauté pan just before serving.
>
> **Storage tip:** These rolls can be stored in the freezer, but they can get sticky and break if you let them touch each other right after rolling. To prevent this, put the freshly rolled nem spaced apart on a baking sheet or platter. Place in the freezer for an hour, then remove them from the tray and transfer to a zip-top bag. Defrost the rolls before frying, patting dry with paper towels if necessary.

Vegan Fried Rolls *Chả giò Ch*

MAKES 10 ROLLS • PREP TIME: 45 MINUTES • COOK TIME: 20 MINUTES

Many Vietnamese people often eat vegan food because of Buddhist influences. It's a common practice for people to pray at Buddhist pagodas and eat vegan food at least twice a month, on the Jrst (new moon) and the Jfteenth (full moon) days of the lunar calendar, the two most important days in a water-cultivated rice culture. The point of people eating vegan on those two days is to have a light spirit by eating all-vegetable meals to avoid taking life. Many restaurants in Vietnam serve delicious vegan food. These vegan rolls are inspired by Hum, the most famous vegetarian restaurant in Saigon.

FOR THE VEGAN SAUCE

2 tablespoons soy sauce

2 tablespoons rice vinegar

2 tablespoons sugar

1½ teaspoons minced hot chile (optional)

FOR THE ROLLS

1 ounce glass noodles

6 ounces king oyster (trumpet) mushrooms, shredded

1 cup shredded carrot

1 small onion, chopped

1 tablespoon soy sauce

1 teaspoon freshly ground black pepper

10 (8-inch) rice paper sheets

Vegetable oil, for frying

To make the vegan sauce

In a bowl, whisk the soy sauce, rice vinegar, and sugar until the sugar dissolves. Add the hot chile (if using) and set aside.

To assemble the rolls

1. Soak the glass noodles in water for 15 minutes. Drain and cut into 1-inch pieces.
2. In a large bowl, combine the noodles, mushrooms, carrot, onion, soy sauce, and pepper.
3. Fill a large bowl with lukewarm water and prepare a flat, dry surface, like a platter or cutting board that is larger than the rice papers.
4. Dip a sheet of rice paper into the bowl. Soak it so it becomes soft but not limp, then remove the paper and gently shake off the excess water. The paper should be flexible enough to fold without cracking. Stretch the rice paper on the flat surface.
5. Place a spoonful of the mushroom mixture on the rice paper. Using your fingers, shape the mixture into a cylinder that stretches toward the sides of the paper.
6. Start rolling from the edge nearest to you toward the center of the rice paper, folding the excess on both sides in toward the center. Roll the paper the rest of the way until tight and even.
7. Repeat with the remaining rolls, leaving space between them to avoid sticking.

To fry the rolls

1. In a medium nonstick sauté pan, pour in the oil to a depth of ¼ inch and heat over high heat until it reaches about 390°F. Check with a thermometer, or by dipping a chopstick into the oil. If the oil sizzles, it's ready. You can also check by lowering a roll into the oil.
2. Reduce the heat to medium and add the rolls, giving them space. Fry until one side is golden. Flip and fry until the other side is golden. Transfer the rolls to

paper towels to drain.

3. Serve immediately with the vegan sauce.

> **Substitution tip:** You can replace the king oyster mushrooms with shiitake, button, or enoki mushrooms.
>
> **Variation tip:** You can also serve these rolls with Peanut Soy Sauce Dip or, if you're not vegan, Sweet and Sour Fish Sauce Dip.

Grilled / Roasted Shrimp Sausage Rolls
Chạo Tôm

MAKES 10 SAUSAGES • PREP TIME: 20 MINUTES • COOK TIME: 25 MINUTES

This dish from the south of Vietnam is traditionally made with sugarcane skewers. But since sugarcane is not available year round in other regions, we sometimes substitute lemongrass skewers, wooden skewers, or no skewers at all (as here). Some friends have even tried them with asparagus "skewers" and the result was delicious! Like many other Vietnamese grilled street dishes, these rolls are delicious cooked over open fire. We don't always have the luxury of space or ventilation to char-grill at home though, so instead we utilize the oven or a nonstick sauté pan. Wrapping the filling in a lettuce leaf with herbs and dipping it in sweet and sour fish sauce or peanut sauce provides a yummy contrast to the savory flavors.

Vegetable oil, for greasing the pan and brushing the sausages

1 large egg white

1 tablespoon fish sauce

1 teaspoon cornstarch

¼ teaspoon freshly ground black pepper

1 pound shrimp, peeled and deveined

1 shallot

1 tablespoon honey

1 cup fresh mint leaves

1 head lettuce

2 recipes Sweet and Sour Fish Sauce Dip

1. Preheat the oven to 450°F.
2. Line a baking sheet with aluminum foil. Grease the foil with vegetable oil.
3. In a large bowl, whisk together the egg white, fish sauce, cornstarch, and pepper. Transfer the mixture to a food processor and add the shrimp and shallot.
4. Pulse 6 times, for about 12 seconds each, pausing for a few seconds in between pulses to prevent the mixture from getting warm. Mix in batches if necessary. The result should be a smooth, fine paste. (If you don't have a food processor, finely chop the shrimp and pound it using a mortar and greased pestle until it becomes a fine paste, 5 to 7 minutes. Then mix the paste well with the fish sauce mixture.)
5. Grease your hands with oil or fill a bowl with water to dip your hands into before and while working the paste. Divide the paste into 10 portions. Form each portion into a sausage shape and place on the prepared baking sheet.
6. Brush the sausages with vegetable oil and bake for 20 minutes. Turn on the broiler.
7. Brush the honey over the sausages and broil them for 3 to 5 minutes.
8. Wrap each shrimp sausage and some mint in a lettuce leaf and serve with the dipping sauce.

Variation tip: These sausages can be served in a vermicelli bowl with herbs and dipping sauce. You can also wrap these rolls in rice paper instead of lettuce leaves.

Ingredient tip: You can use frozen shrimp for this recipe. Leave the shrimp at room temperature for 5 minutes, then rinse under running water for 1 minute. Drain well. Break the shrimp into pieces before processing.

Cooking tip: You can deep-fry the sausages if you like.

Pan-Seared Beef With Mustard Green Rolls
Bò Cuốn Lá Cải

SERVES 2 • PREP TIME: 20 MINUTES + 30 MINUTES TO MARINATE • COOK TIME: 7 MINUTES

This dish is very popular in the ubiquitous beer gardens of Hanoi. The spiciness of mustard greens complements beef very well, and when you add some beer, friends, and sultry tropical night air, it's downright magical. The beef can be boiled with ginger or grilled; in this recipe I opt for a convenient indoor pan-searing method. It's fast and the beef comes out very tender. Beef cut with a little fat works best for this recipe. Vietnamese people like to add slices of young green bananas for tartness, but mango or cucumber is also good. This dish is nice with sweet and sour fish sauce, and there should be some ginger in the sauce to give warmth (yang) to the beef, which is considered a cool (yin) food.

1 pound boneless ribeye steak, cut into ½-inch-thick strips

5 garlic cloves, lightly smashed

1 (2-inch) piece ginger, half lightly smashed and half peeled and minced

3 tablespoons vegetable oil, divided

1 tablespoon soy sauce

¼ teaspoon salt

1 teaspoon freshly ground black pepper

2 recipes Sweet and Sour Fish Sauce Dip

15 to 20 mustard green leaves

1 pineapple, peeled, cored, and cut into thin slices or thin wedges

1 mango, peeled, pitted, and cut into thin slices

1. In a large bowl, toss together the beef, garlic, the smashed ginger, 1 tablespoon of oil, the soy sauce, salt, and pepper. Cover and let marinate at room temperature for 30 minutes.
2. Heat a sauté pan over high heat. You can check by spraying a few drops of water into the pan. When the water evaporates, swirl in the remaining 2 tablespoons of oil to spread it evenly. Add the beef and cook until browned on the bottom, about 2 minutes. Turn the beef to brown the other side, about 2 minutes. Remove the pan from the heat.
3. Add the minced ginger to the fish sauce dip and mix well.
4. Wrap a portion of beef, pineapple, and mango slices into each mustard green leaf, and serve with the fish sauce dip.

Substitution tip: *You can substitute lettuce leaves for the mustard greens. If you do, add some Asian/Thai basil and mint to the rolls for more depth of flavor.*

Grilled Beef in Wild Betel Leaf Rolls *Bò Cuốn Lá Lốt*

MAKES 15 ROLLS • PREP TIME: 25 MINUTES • COOK TIME: 18 MINUTES

Lá lốt (wild betel leaf) is well loved in Vietnamese cuisine because of its wide-ranging medicinal properties. Thought to warm up the body and aid in digestion, it has a flavorful spiciness and aroma considered therapeutic. In northern home-cooked meals, we simply wrap the betel leaves around minced pork, then fry the rolls, dip them in pure fish sauce, and eat them with steamed rice. In the central and southern regions, people use ground beef instead of pork and sprinkle roasted peanuts on the rolls before serving. This dish is also a popular street food in both regions. Vendors usually char-grill these rolls, but most home cooks opt to roast or pan-fry them.

3 tablespoons light sesame oil or vegetable oil, divided

8 ounces boneless ribeye steak, cut into ¾-inch cubes

3 garlic cloves, lightly smashed

1 shallot, lightly smashed

1 tablespoon minced lemongrass (optional)

1 tablespoon fish sauce

1 teaspoon freshly ground black pepper

½ teaspoon five-spice powder

15 wild betel leaves

¼ cup roasted peanuts, coarsely chopped

2 recipes Sweet and Sour Fish Sauce Dip

1. Preheat the oven to 425°F. Line a baking sheet with aluminum foil. Grease the foil with 1 tablespoon of sesame oil.

2. In a food processor, combine the beef, garlic, shallot, lemongrass (if using), 1 tablespoon of oil, fish sauce, pepper, and five-spice powder. Process the mixture for about a minute. (If you don't have a food processor, buy ground beef or finely chop the beef cubes with a cleaver.)

3. Remove the betel leaf stems and wash the leaves thoroughly. Drain well and pat dry with paper towels. Place the shiny darker green side down, with the wider end of the heart-shaped leaf closest to you. Place a spoonful of the beef mixture about a third of the way from the edge of the leaf closest to you. Using your fingers, shape the meat into a cylinder almost as wide as the leaf. Begin rolling tightly from the edge closest to you, without folding in the sides. Roll completely.

4. Place the rolls on the foil, seam-side down. Brush the rolls with the remaining 1 tablespoon of sesame oil. Bake for 15 minutes.

5. Turn on the broiler and broil the rolls for 3 minutes.

6. Transfer the rolls to a plate. Sprinkle with the roasted peanuts and serve with the fish sauce dip.

Variation tip: Try serving these rolls alongside rice vermicelli.

Cooking tip: You can pan-fry these rolls in a thin layer of oil (3 to 4 tablespoons) in a medium nonstick sauté pan. Fry over medium heat until one side browns nicely, about 5 minutes, then turn and fry until the other side browns, about 4 minutes. Don't overstuff the rolls with meat, because they might break when the meat expands during cooking.

Roasted Fish With Dill, Ginger, and Scallion Rolls *Cá Cuốn*

SERVES 2 • PREP TIME: 20 MINUTES + 30 MINUTES TO MARINATE • COOK TIME: 35 MINUTES

Although as a child I enjoyed this dish in its aromatic steamed form, steaming only works well with fish that is fresh off the hook, that still jumps around in your kitchen sink! Since I don't have that luxury, I opt to roast my fish — it's equally delicious and easier to prepare. This recipe works best with firm, white-fleshed fish such as red snapper, mackerel, sea bass, hake, or mahi mahi. But don't feel beholden to these suggestions — just pick a white-fleshed fish that you like, or one that is available.

1 (2-pound) red snapper, cleaned, gutted, and scaled

1 (2-inch) piece ginger, peeled and minced

1 shallot, minced

5 garlic cloves, minced

1 tablespoon minced hot chile

2 tablespoons fish sauce

4 tablespoons light sesame oil

¼ teaspoon salt

1 teaspoon freshly ground black pepper

10 scallions, cut into 2-inch pieces, divided

10 dill sprigs, cut into 2-inch pieces, divided

5 lemongrass stalks, smashed

8 (8-inch) rice paper rolls or 1 head lettuce

1 cucumber, shredded

½ pineapple, cut into thin slices or wedges

1 cup fresh cilantro leaves

1 cup fresh mint leaves

3 recipes Sweet and Sour Fish Sauce Dip

1. Cut 3 diagonal slices partway into both sides of the fish.
2. In a bowl, whisk together the ginger, shallot, garlic, chile, fish sauce, 2 tablespoons of oil, salt, and pepper. Rub this mixture on the outside and inside of the fish. Stuff the fish with half of the scallions and half of the dill. Cover and set aside to marinate for 30 minutes.
3. Preheat the oven to 425°F.
4. Line a baking sheet with aluminum foil. Grease the foil with 1 tablespoon of oil. Spread out the lemongrass in a single layer. Place the fish on the lemongrass. Top with the remaining scallions and dill. Drizzle the fish with the remaining 1 tablespoon of oil. Bake for 25 minutes.
5. Turn on the broiler. Broil the fish for 5 minutes.
6. If using rice paper rolls, fill a large bowl with lukewarm water and prepare a flat, dry surface, like a platter or cutting board that is larger than the rice papers. Dip a sheet of rice paper into the bowl. Soak it so it becomes soft but not limp, then remove the paper and gently shake off the excess water. The paper should be flexible enough to fold without cracking. Stretch the rice paper on the flat surface.
7. To form the rolls, use a rice paper or lettuce leaf to wrap up a piece of fish along with some cucumber, pineapple, cilantro, and mint. Serve with the fish sauce dip.

Substitution tip: *Instead of lemongrass stalks, you can use ¼-inch-thick ginger slices. Lightly smash the ginger slices to release their fragrance before placing them on the foil.*

Ingredient tip: *You can also use fish fillets or fish steaks for this recipe. Adjust the cooking time depending on the thickness of the fish.*

Cooking tip: *Traditionally we don't cut the fish into smaller pieces before serving. Instead, we each break off pieces with chopsticks as we're eating. However, you can cut the fish into bite-size pieces to make it easier to share or handle.*

Shrimp and Mango Salad

Chapter Three

Nộm/Gỏi
SALADS

Fish Sauce Salad Dressing *Nước Mắm Trộn Gỏi/Nộm*

Shrimp and Mango Salad *Gỏi Tôm Xoài*

Green Papaya Salad *Nộm Đu Đủ*

Chicken and Cabbage Salad *Gỏi Gà Xé Phay Bắp Cải*

Chicken and Onion Salad *Gỏi Gà Xé Phay Hành Tây*

Kohlrabi and Carrot Salad *Nộm Su Hào Cà Rốt*

Shrimp and Pomelo Salad *Gỏi Bưởi*

Banana Blossom Salad *Nộm Hoa Chuối*

Calamari Salad *Gỏi Mực*

Pan-Seared Beef and Watercress Salad *Bò Trộn Cải Xoong*

King Oyster Mushroom Salad *Gỏi Nấm Đùi Gà*

Cucumber and Tofu Salad   *Nộm Dưa Leo Và Đậu Phụ*

Nộm (the northern word for salad; gỏi is the same thing in the central and southern regions) always brings me back to summer afternoons on our front porch. The air was sultry and thick, and it was too hot to cook in the kitchen. That weather called for something fresh, crunchy, flavorful, and requiring a minimal amount of cooking. My mother used to make vegetable nộm, and my job was to crack peanut shells while she prepared the vegetables and mixed the dressing. It's very humid in the North, so we kept the peanut shells on and cracked them right before cooking. After roasting the peanuts, my mother wrapped them in cloth or newspaper so the peanut skins would slide off more easily when we rubbed them later. My favorite job was to blow the peanut skins out of the colander. They flew into the air like tiny firecrackers.

The key to a good Vietnamese nộm/gỏi is fresh herbs and sweet and sour dressing. Other than that, as with rolls, just pick the seasonal and local ingredients that you like and adjust the amount of vegetables and protein to taste. As we Vietnamese often say, what we eat is based on the sky—meaning weather and season—and the land, meaning the location or region. You can add [Crispy Fried Shallots](#) as a topping to all salads in this chapter, but this is a modern addition and optional.

Fish Sauce Salad Dressing *Nước Mắm Trộn Gỏi/Nôm*

SERVES 2 • PREP TIME: 10 MINUTES

This salad dressing is similar to the **Sweet and Sour Fish Sauce Dip.** *However, we don't add water in the salad dressing version because that can make the vegetables in the salad soggy. This delicious dressing can be used with all the salad recipes in this chapter. Conveniently, you can store this dressing in a glass jar in the refrigerator for up to a month—just reserve the garlic and chile until just before serving, to keep their flavors distinct and the dressing from becoming too spicy over time.*

- 2½ tablespoons freshly squeezed lime juice
- 2 tablespoons fish sauce
- 3 tablespoons sugar
- 1 tablespoon minced garlic
- 1½ teaspoons minced hot chile

Whisk the lime juice, fish sauce, and sugar until the sugar fully dissolves. Add the garlic and chile and serve.

> **Substitution tip:** *You can substitute rice vinegar for the lime juice. Other kinds of vinegar work, but depending on how sour they are, you might have to adjust the sugar amount.*

Shrimp and Mango Salad *Gỏi Tôm Xoài*

SERVES 2 • PREP TIME: 20 MINUTES • COOK TIME: 10 MINUTES

This salad originated in the south of Vietnam, home to the best mangos, but it's popular all over the country now. My uncle, who lives in a Saigon suburb, has several mango trees in his garden, and my aunt usually makes this dish for me when I visit in the summer. My aunt is truly a mango master! She makes soup and pickles from young, green sour mangos and pudding from the juicy, sweet ripe ones. This recipe, which I learned from her, calls for medium-ripe mangos.

1 teaspoon salt

1 pound large shrimp

1 medium-ripe mango, peeled, pitted, and shredded

1 (2-inch) piece ginger, peeled and minced

1 recipe Fish Sauce Salad Dressing

½ cup fresh mint leaves, coarsely chopped

½ cup roasted peanuts, coarsely chopped

1. Fill a saucepan with water. Add the salt and bring to a boil over high heat.
2. Add the shrimp, cover, and return to a boil. Uncover and cook for 2 more minutes.
3. Transfer the shrimp to a bowl of ice water to let the shrimp firm up and retain their pink color. Peel and devein the shrimp.
4. In a mixing bowl, combine the shrimp, mango, and ginger. Drizzle with the salad dressing and toss. Add most of the chopped mint (leaving some for the garnish) and mix well.

5. Divide the salad between two plates, sprinkle with the peanuts, and garnish with the remaining mint leaves. Serve.

> ***Variation tip:*** *Instead of roasted peanuts, give this recipe a little twist by using other kinds of nuts like cashews, almonds, or walnuts.*

Green Papaya Salad

Nộm Đu Đủ

SERVES 2 • PREP TIME: 30 MINUTES

This dish is popular throughout Vietnam, but even more so in the central region where I live now, because the sunny weather and the soil are perfect for papaya trees. In fact, I threw papaya seeds in my front yard and somehow they started growing like weeds in both my front and back yards! Green papaya has a natural sweetness, and this crunchy, fresh salad complements any meat dish.

½ small green papaya, peeled, seeded, and shredded

1 small carrot, peeled and shredded (optional)

1 teaspoon salt

1 recipe Fish Sauce Salad Dressing

½ cup fresh mint leaves, coarsely chopped

½ cup fresh cilantro leaves, coarsely chopped

½ cup fresh Vietnamese balm leaves, coarsely chopped (optional)

½ cup roasted peanuts, coarsely chopped

1. In a bowl, combine the papaya, carrot, and salt. Gently squeeze the mixture with your fingers for 1 to 2 minutes. Let sit for 10 minutes.
2. Rinse the papaya and carrot mixture under running water. Drain well, then squeeze out the excess water with your hands or a cheesecloth.
3. Return the papaya and carrot to the bowl. Drizzle with the dressing and toss.
4. Add the chopped mint, cilantro, and balm leaves, and toss again. Divide the salad between two plates and sprinkle with the chopped peanuts. Serve.

Variation tip: *Thailand has its own version of papaya salad, with string beans and tomatoes. You can also add beef jerky, grilled or boiled shrimp, or grilled* *beef to this salad.*

Chicken and Cabbage Salad *Gỏi Gà Xé Ph Bắp Cải*

SERVES 2 • PREP TIME: 20 MINUTES • COOK TIME: 20 MINUTES

When I was small, our next-door neighbor was from Huế, a city in the central region. From time to time I would hear him talk to my grandparents about a strange dish called gà xé phay. I knew gà, chicken, and I knew xé, which is to tear or rip something with your hands, but the rest didn't make any sense to me. I ate this dish many times without understanding the name. One day I learned from my linguistics class that phay is a really old word meaning "into pieces." So this dish simply means shredded chicken.

- 1 pound chicken drumsticks (or any part of the chicken that you like), skin removed
- 1 (2-inch) piece ginger, lightly smashed
- 1 shallot, lightly smashed, or ½ onion, thinly sliced
- 1¼ teaspoons salt, divided
- ½ teaspoon freshly ground black pepper
- ½ small cabbage, shredded as thinly as possible
- 1 recipe [Fish Sauce Salad Dressing](#)
- 1 cup fresh Vietnamese or regular mint leaves, coarsely chopped
- ½ cup roasted peanuts, coarsely chopped

1. In a saucepan, combine the chicken, ginger, shallot, and 1 teaspoon of salt. Pour in enough water to cover the chicken. Bring the water to a boil over medium heat. Turn off the heat and let the chicken sit in the hot water for about 15 minutes. Check for doneness by poking a chopstick or fork through the meat. If

there's no pink juice, then the chicken is done. Transfer the chicken to a bowl of ice water to cool.

2. Shred the meat with a knife or your hands. Season the chicken with the remaining ¼ teaspoon of salt and the pepper.

3. In a bowl, toss the cabbage with half of the dressing. Add the chicken, then drizzle on the remaining dressing and toss. Add the chopped mint and toss again.

4. Divide the salad between two plates and sprinkle with the roasted peanuts. Serve.

***Ingredient tip:** Buy savoy cabbage, if possible, because it's softer. You can also mix white and purple cabbages for added color.*

Chicken and Onion Salad — Gỏi Gà Xé Ph Hành Tây

SERVES 2 • PREP TIME: 20 MINUTES • MARINATE TIME: 10 MINUTES • COOK TIME: 20 MINUTES

Gà xé phay originated in the central region but is popular throughout the country. Characteristic of that region, there are layers of spiciness in this salad from the black pepper, hot chiles, and Vietnamese mint (rau răm), which is a strong herb. However, when paired with the other ingredients, each bite strikes that perfect balance of sweet, sour, spicy, and salty flavors, and of tender chicken and crunchy vegetables.

1 pound chicken drumsticks (or other chicken part you like)

1 (2-inch) piece ginger, lightly smashed

1 shallot, lightly smashed

2¼ teaspoons salt, divided

2 medium onions, halved and thinly sliced

1 tablespoon vinegar (any type)

1 tablespoon sugar

½ teaspoon freshly ground black pepper

1 recipe Fish Sauce Salad Dressing

½ cup Vietnamese mint or regular mint, coarsely chopped

½ cup roasted peanuts, coarsely chopped

1. In a saucepan, combine the chicken, ginger, shallot, and 1 teaspoon of salt. Pour in enough water to cover the chicken. Bring the water to a boil over medium heat. Turn off the heat and let the chicken sit in the hot water for about 15 minutes. Check for doneness by poking a chopstick or fork through the meat. If

there's no pink juice, then the chicken is done. Transfer the chicken to a bowl of ice water to cool.

2. Meanwhile, soak the onion slices in a bowl of ice water for 10 minutes. Drain well. Add 1 teaspoon of salt. Mix well and gently squeeze with your fingers for about 2 minutes. Rinse the onion under running water, then squeeze out the excess water with your hands or a cheesecloth. Transfer the onion slices to a bowl and season with the vinegar and sugar. Set aside to marinate for 10 minutes.

3. Shred the chicken meat with your hands or with a knife. Season the chicken with the remaining ¼ teaspoon of salt and the pepper.

4. In a bowl, toss the chicken with half of the dressing. Add the onion and remaining dressing and toss again. Add the chopped mint and mix well.

5. Divide the salad between two plates and sprinkle with the roasted peanuts. Serve.

Ingredient tip: Any kind of onion will work with this recipe, but the ideal choice is sweet onions. True to their name, they are a lot less pungent than other kinds. If you do use sweet onions, skip the salting, rinsing, and squeezing part in step 2 and just let them marinate in the vinegar and sugar.

Kohlrabi and Carrot Salad *Nộm Su Hào Cà Rốt*

SERVES 2 • PREP TIME: 30 MINUTES

This dish is a must-have at Tết (Vietnamese New Year) meals in the North. Kohlrabi, brought to us by the French, is tastiest in early spring, just in time for the New Year. The fresh, crunchy texture of this salad, together with the signature sweet, sour, salty, and spicy flavors, is a perfect complement to meat dishes. This recipe comes from my mother, who makes this salad in a giant bowl for more than thirty of us every Tết.

2 kohlrabi (about 1 pound total), peeled and shredded

1 small carrot, peeled and shredded

1 tablespoon salt

2 tablespoons freshly squeezed lime juice

2 tablespoons sugar

½ teaspoon minced hot chile

1 cup fresh Vietnamese balm leaves, coarsely chopped

1 cup fresh Thai/Asian basil leaves, coarsely chopped

½ cup roasted peanuts, coarsely chopped

1. In a large bowl, toss together the kohlrabi, carrot, and salt. Gently squeeze with your fingers for about 1 minute, then let sit for 10 minutes. Squeeze out the excess water with your hands or a cheesecloth. Transfer the kohlrabi and carrot to a bowl.

2. In a small bowl, whisk the lime juice, sugar, and hot chile until the sugar dissolves.

3. Drizzle the kohlrabi and carrot with the lime juice mixture and toss. Just before serving, mix in the herbs and sprinkle with the peanuts.

> **Substitution tip:** Mint and cilantro are good stand-ins if you can't find balm leaves and Thai/Asian basil.
>
> **Variation tip:** You can use [Fish Sauce Salad Dressing](#) instead of the lime juice mixture. If you do, reduce the salt from 1 tablespoon to 1 teaspoon. Also, rinse the vegetables under running water after salting, then squeeze out the excess water.
>
> **Storage tip:** This salad can be made in advance and kept in the refrigerator for a day. Reserve the herbs and peanuts until right before serving to prevent the herbs from turning gray and the peanuts from getting soft.

Shrimp and Pomelo Salad *Gỏi Bưởi*

PREP TIME: 20 MINUTES • COOK TIME: 10 MINUTES

Our pomelo tree always had so many giant green fruits hanging from it that even though we gave them away as presents, there were still too many fresh fruit to eat. Rather than let them rot, my grandmother preserved the fruits by putting a little bit of hydrated lime on the pomelos and placing them under our beds, where they would stay fresh for several months. That way, I got to enjoy pomelo as a fruit for desserts and snacks for much of the year. However, I got the pleasure of eating it in a savory dish like this salad only after I visited Vietnam's southern region for the first time.

- ½ teaspoon salt
- 1 (2-inch) piece ginger, lightly smashed
- 1 pound jumbo shrimp
- ½ pomelo, peeled and cut into bite-size pieces
- 1 recipe Fish Sauce Salad Dressing
- 2 cups mixed fresh mint leaves, cilantro leaves, and/or Asian/Thai basil leaves, coarsely chopped
- ½ cup roasted peanuts, coarsely chopped

1. Fill a saucepan with water. Add the salt and ginger and bring to a boil over high heat.
2. Add the shrimp, cover, and return to a boil. Uncover and cook for 2 more minutes.
3. Transfer the shrimp to a bowl of ice water to let the shrimp firm up and retain their pink color. Peel and devein the shrimp.

4. In a bowl, combine the shrimp, pomelo, and salad dressing and mix well. Add the mint, cilantro, and basil mixture and mix again. Just before serving, sprinkle with the peanuts.

Ingredient tip: *Pomelos look like oversized grapefruits, but they're sweeter and less watery. They're usually available from November to March in Asian markets, and I've also seen them at Costco, Whole Foods, and even some small grocery stores. Make sure to remove all the white pith, because it's bitter.*

The Versatile Pomelo

Many of my childhood memories involve the trusty pomelo tree in my grandparents' garden. In the spring, my grandmother would pick the fragrant white blossoms to steep in tea and to make my favorite pudding dessert. In the summer, she cooked up an herbal shampoo mixture using pomelo peel and herbs. She said the oil from pomelo peel made hair shiny and left a pleasant scent.

I used to collect pomelo seeds with the other children in the neighborhood, dry them, and fashion them into chains that would adorn our torches for the mid-autumn festival parade. The seeds burn for a long time, plus they smell delicious and make a funny pop as they burn. The fall was also the beginning of the fruit season. We enjoyed pomelos in many dishes and desserts, and my grandmother found ways to stretch their season even farther.

Banana Blossom Salad *Nộm H Chuối*

SERVES 2 • PREP TIME: 30 MINUTES

Banana blossoms might be too exotic to be sourced easily in the West, but I still want to share the recipe for this salad because it's a special-occasion dish in our cuisine and worth a try if you can find the ingredients. I've seen banana blossoms in New York's Chinatown many times, so it isn't an impossible task in cities with large Asian communities. Give your nearest Asian market a look.

1 banana blossom

2 tablespoons freshly squeezed lime juice

1 tablespoon salt

1 cup fresh cilantro leaves, coarsely chopped

1 cup fresh mint leaves, coarsely chopped

1 cup fresh Vietnamese mint leaves, coarsely chopped (optional)

1 cup fresh Asian/Thai basil leaves, coarsely chopped (optional)

1 recipe Fish Sauce Salad Dressing

½ cup roasted peanuts, coarsely chopped

1. Peel the outer petals of the banana blossom until the little flowers inside, which are bananas-to-be and look like flowers themselves, are visible. Keep the fresh-looking ones, and discard any gray or brown ones.
2. Fill a large bowl with water. Stir in the lime juice and salt.
3. Wash and cut the blossoms into very thin slices, the thinner, the better. Let the slices soak in the salt and lime juice water for 15 minutes. Rinse well and drain well.

4. Transfer the blossom slices to a bowl. Add the cilantro, mint, and basil, drizzle with the salad dressing, and toss. Sprinkle with the peanuts before serving.

Variation tip: *This traditional meatless version works as a side dish in a shared meal. You can add chicken to make it a main dish.*

Banana Blossoms

For those of you who have never seen a banana blossom before, it looks like a giant purple magnolia bud. Much like Native Americans with the buffalo, the Vietnamese cook makes use of all parts of a banana tree — nothing goes to waste. We use the leaves as molds for making sausages and bánh. Thanks to their flexibility and endurance, the stems are used as strings or straps to bunch vegetables together in the marketplace. And we have many dishes cooked with young green bananas, which taste like a more flavorful version of potato.

Banana Blossom Salad is another dish that rekindles my childhood memories. If there was a banana blossom on the trees when relatives visited, my grandmother would make this delicious salad. This was for special guests only, because we preferred to leave the blossom on the tree to grow into fruit. I loved it every time my grandmother made this salad. Not only did I get to eat it, but I could also keep the otherwise useless outside petals as toys. I dropped them into our pond and they floated around like little purple boats.

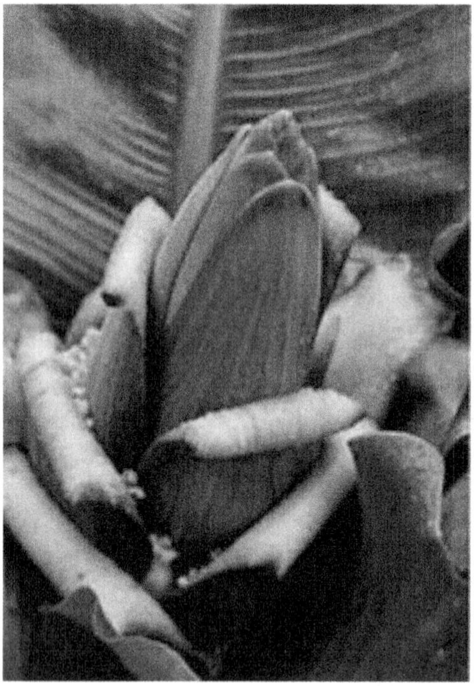

Calamari Salad *Gỏi Mực*

SERVES 2 • PREP TIME: 15 MINUTES • COOK TIME: 10 MINUTES

Usually, small restaurants in Vietnam are also the owner's home, and the owners will often eat their meals at another table if the restaurant is not too busy. One day I saw the owners of this beach restaurant eating a colorful plate of food, and I couldn't help asking what it was. In their typically kind central region way, they offered me a small bowl to try. It was so delicious that I asked for the recipe, and it has become one of my favorite dishes.

1 (2-inch) piece ginger, peeled, two-thirds thinly sliced and one-third minced

1 pound calamari (body only, not tentacles), cleaned

½ cup beer

1 tablespoon minced hot chile

1 recipe Fish Sauce Salad Dressing

1 celery stalk (optional)

½ cucumber (preferably English), shredded

1 cup mixed fresh Asian/Thai basil, mint, and cilantro leaves, coarsely chopped

½ cup roasted sesame seeds (optional)

1. Spread the smashed ginger slices in a layer in a small saucepan. Add the calamari, then pour the beer over it. Cover and cook over high heat until the calamari is ivory-colored, 5 to 7 minutes.

2. Remove the calamari and cut it into ½-inch rings with a knife or scissors. In a bowl, toss the calamari rings with the chile. Drizzle with half of the salad dressing and toss again. Set aside.

3. If desired, cut the celery stalk into 3-inch chunks. Using a peeler, shave off thin slices.

4. In a large bowl, combine the celery, cucumber, and minced ginger. Drizzle on the remaining half of the salad dressing and toss. Add the calamari and basil, mint, and cilantro mixture and mix well. Sprinkle with the roasted sesame seeds (if using) and serve.

Ingredient tip: Choose small calamari (1½ to 2 inches wide). Bigger ones might be a little too chewy for this salad and require a different cutting technique.

Pan-Seared Beef and Watercress Salad *Bò Trộn Cải X ng*

SERVES 2 • PREP TIME: 25 MINUTES • COOK TIME: 3 MINUTES

Along with kohlrabi, watercress is another vegetable that the French brought to Vietnam during the colonial period. Its name in Vietnamese is cải xoong, pronounced "kaisong" and derived from cresson *in French. This dish originated in Dalat, a beautiful city in the Central Highlands region of Vietnam that was a vacation town for French bureaucrats at the time. The mild climate there, similar to parts of northern Europe or the northwestern United States, makes it a great city for growing Western vegetables and flowers, so watercress is one of its specialties.*

8 ounces boneless ribeye steak, thinly sliced against the grain

3 garlic cloves, lightly smashed

1 (2-inch) piece ginger, lightly smashed

1 tablespoon minced lemongrass (optional)

3 tablespoons light sesame oil, divided

1 tablespoon soy sauce

1 teaspoon sugar

1 teaspoon freshly ground black pepper

1 bunch fresh watercress, roots trimmed if necessary

1 recipe Fish Sauce Salad Dressing

1. In a large bowl, toss together the beef, garlic, ginger, lemongrass (if using), 1 tablespoon of oil, soy sauce, sugar, and pepper.

2. Cut the watercress into 3- to 4-inch pieces and put them in a bowl. Drizzle with half of the salad dressing and toss.

3. Heat a sauté pan over high heat. Swirl in the remaining 2 tablespoons of oil to spread it evenly. Add the beef slices and cook until nicely brown, about 1 minute. Turn and cook the other side for 1 minute. Transfer the beef to the bowl of watercress. Add the remaining salad dressing and toss. Serve.

Variation tip: This pan-seared beef also pairs well with the mango, green papaya, kohlrabi, and cucumber salads in this chapter.

King Oyster Mushroom Salad *Gỏi Nấm Đùi Gà*

SERVES 2 • PREP TIME: 15 MINUTES • COOK TIME: 5 MINUTES

Many Vietnamese go to a pagoda to pray for their health on the first and fifteenth of every month of the lunar calendar. People go even if they're not Buddhist because they say the serenity of pagodas gives them peace of mind. Many pagodas offer free vegan food for visitors on those two days. My aunt taught me how to make this dish after she tried it at a pagoda near her house in the southern countryside.

FOR THE DRESSING

1½ tablespoons soy sauce

1½ tablespoons rice vinegar

1½ tablespoons sugar

1 tablespoon minced ginger

1½ tablespoons toasted sesame oil

FOR THE SALAD

1 teaspoon salt

3 king oyster (trumpet) mushrooms (about 1 pound), trimmed and shredded

1 (2-inch) piece ginger, peeled, half lightly smashed and half minced

½ cup fresh Vietnamese mint or cilantro leaves, chopped

½ cup roasted peanuts, coarsely chopped

To make the dressing

In a bowl, whisk the soy sauce, rice vinegar, sugar, and ginger until the sugar dissolves. Stir in the sesame oil. Set aside.

To make the salad

1. Bring a generous amount of water to a boil over high heat. Add the salt. Add the mushrooms and smashed ginger and blanch (see here) for 2 minutes. Transfer the mushrooms to a bowl of ice cold water and discard the ginger. Drain the mushrooms well.

2. In a bowl, combine the mushrooms and minced ginger. Drizzle with the salad dressing and toss. Add the mint and toss again. Sprinkle with the roasted peanuts and serve.

> **Substitution tip:** *You can substitute other kinds of mushrooms like enoki or clamshell (also known as beech or shimeji mushrooms) for king oyster mushrooms.*

Cucumber and Tofu Salad _Nộm Dưa o Và Đậu Phụ_

SERVES 2 • PREP TIME: 20 MINUTES • COOK TIME: 12 MINUTES

I first ate this salad when it was prepared by the mother of a college friend. It was amazingly refreshing and delicious. When I asked my friend's mother what spices she had used, she was surprised and replied, "What? How can you not know? You're supposed to figure it out yourself when eating it." It was a very reasonable response in Vietnamese. And she was right—I should have known. She ended up telling me what was in the salad.

FOR THE DRESSING

1½ tablespoons soy sauce

1½ tablespoons rice vinegar

1½ tablespoons sugar

1 tablespoon minced ginger

1½ tablespoons toasted sesame oil

FOR THE SALAD

1 (10-ounce) block firm tofu

¼ cup vegetable oil

1 English cucumber, shredded

¼ teaspoon salt

1 cup fresh mint leaves, chopped

1 cup fresh cilantro leaves, chopped

1 cup fresh Vietnamese balm leaves, chopped (optional)

½ cup roasted peanuts, coarsely chopped

To make the dressing

In a bowl, whisk the soy sauce, rice vinegar, sugar, and ginger until the sugar dissolves. Stir in the sesame oil. Set aside.

To make the salad

1. Pat the tofu dry with a paper towel, the drier, the better to reduce spattering when frying. Halve the tofu lengthwise and then cut it crosswise into 8 pieces.
2. Heat a medium sauté pan over medium-high heat. Swirl in the oil to spread it evenly. Add the tofu and fry until golden on the bottom, about 7 minutes. Flip over and fry the other side until golden, about 5 minutes.
3. Transfer to a bowl. Drizzle with half of the dressing and gently toss. Set aside. When the tofu cools, cut each piece in half with scissors.
4. In a bowl, toss the cucumber and salt and let sit for 5 minutes. Add the remaining salad dressing and mix well. Add the tofu and chopped herbs and mix well. Sprinkle with the peanuts and serve.

Ingredient tip: If you use other kinds of cucumber, seed them before mixing. Otherwise the salad and tofu will get soggy from cucumber juice.

Grilled Pork Bánh Mì

Chapter Four

Bánh
FLOUR- AND STARCH-BASED FOODS

Steamed Rice Crêpe Rolls *Bánh Cuốn*

Crispy Savory Crêpes *Bánh Xèo*

Chicken Curry Bánh Mì *Bánh Mì Cà-Ri Gà*

Vegan Curry Bánh Mì *Bánh Mì Cà-Ri Chay*

Baguette with Beef in Red Wine Stew *Bánh Mì Bò Sốt Vang*

Homemade Mayonnaise *Sốt Mai-ô-ne*

Carrot and Daikon Pickles *Đồ Chua*

Grilled Pork Bánh Mì *Bánh Mì Heo Nướng*

Grilled Chicken Bánh Mì *Bánh Mì Gà Nướng*

Pineapple Shrimp Bánh Mì *Bánh Mì Kẹp Tôm*

Char Síu Pork Bánh Mì *Bánh Mì Thịt Xá Xíu*

Bánh (pronounced "bang" with a rising tone) is a Vietnamese word that refers to flour- and starch-based foods. English has many words for baked goods, such as cake, pie, doughnut, crêpe, bread, bun, and muffin, but in the Vietnamese language they're all one word: bánh. There are savory bánh like the ones in this chapter and sweet bánh like those in [chapter 9](). Most of our traditional bánh are made from rice flour (good news for the gluten-intolerant!), and they're often wrapped in banana leaves which not only function as a mold to shape the bánh, but also add an herbal aroma to the food. Many traditional bánh are very labor-intensive to prepare, so they are made at home perhaps just once a year to celebrate special occasions. For this reason they also tend to be eaten more on the street, so they often serve as snacks or a light meal—Vietnamese fast food!

The most internationally known Vietnamese bánh is bánh mì or wheat bánh; resembling a baguette, this bread obviously comes from the French, but ours is a Vietnamese adaptation. Whether it is by virtue of our wheat, yeast, or cooking methods, Vietnamese bánh mì crust is much thinner and crispier than the French baguette, and the inside is airy and fluffy so we can add fillings. Bánh mì has been a popular street food for a long, long time—you can see bánh mì carts almost everywhere in Vietnam. Typical bánh mì vendors spend their time making the fillings and, during the day, send a runner to the bakery to pick up still-warm baguettes. In fact, after the bakeries close, many people buy plain baguettes at the bánh mì stand, asking for "bánh mì không," *không* being the Vietnamese word for "nothing" or "air."

Traditional bánh mì fillings are slow-cooked Vietnamese versions of fast food: pâté, pork sausage, cilantro, and cucumber or pickles. However, today there are even more gourmet choices in Vietnam.

There are two common ways of eating bánh mì in Vietnam. We dip (*chấm*) bánh mì in stew, or fill (*kẹp*) bánh mì with pickles, herbs, sauces (chili, mayonnaise), and meat or pâté. Sometimes we even do both, depending on personal preferences. You can find good bánh mì kẹp anywhere in Vietnam, but the ones in Đà Nẵng and Hội An in the central region are believed to be the tastiest. The baguettes in those places are smaller and crispier, and the sauces have more complex flavors.

We don't make baguettes at home for several reasons. First, it costs less than nine cents to buy a warm, crispy baguette fresh out of the oven at the bakery. And second, few homes have ovens, with traditional wood fire still a primary means of cooking for many Vietnamese. However, sometimes we like to pick up some plain baguettes and make stew or meat filling at home, because the quality of homemade filling may be better than what you can get from a street vendor.

Timeless Treks to Aunt Bánh Cuon

When I was small, every morning my mom would give me an allowance for breakfast, usually enough to buy a baguette or a sesame doughnut. On the weekend, however, she would increase it tenfold so I could take my little brother on my green bicycle to our favorite bánh cuốn vendor at the local market. Two miles was quite a long distance for a 10-year-old driving a 4-year-old, but I didn't mind because bánh cuốn was waiting. We loved watching the seller make bánh cuốn—it was like a magic trick to us. We called her Aunt Bánh Cuốn. She had a steamy pot of boiling water with a cloth screen wrapped around it. She would ladle the batter onto the screen, cover the pot, and five seconds later, the crêpe was done. She then put a spoonful of pork and mushroom filling on the crêpe and quickly rolled it. After five crêpes were ready on the plate, she would cut them into bite-size pieces and top them with crispy fried shallots. My brother and I shared that small plate and a tiny bowl of dipping sauce. We tried to eat slowly so that it would last forever.

Steamed Rice Crêpe Rolls *Bánh Cuốn*

SERVES 4 • PREP TIME: 30 MINUTES • COOK TIME: 45 MINUTES

Bánh cuốn is a classic northern delicacy. You can find these rolls everywhere — on the streets, in local markets — and there are even villages that specialize in making bánh cuốn. People usually eat bánh cuốn for breakfast, but some places serve it all day long. Besides the pork and mushroom versions, plain ones are served with cinnamon pork sausages or barbecued pork. The dipping sauce for bánh cuốn is simple, like the basic fish sauce dip but without garlic. As northerners brought this dish farther south, people added cucumber, bean sprouts, and herbs, and the crêpes got thicker.

This recipe calls for a small nonstick sauté pan — about 8 inches in diameter is ideal. Be patient; the first few crêpes might either come out too thick or tear apart, but after the first few tries, you'll get the hang of it.

FOR THE SAUCE

½ cup water

3 tablespoons fish sauce

3 tablespoons rice vinegar or freshly squeezed lime juice

3 tablespoons sugar

Fresh hot chile slices (optional)

FOR THE BATTER

1 (14.1-ounce) package bánh cuốn flour

4¼ cups water

¼ cup vegetable oil

FOR THE FILLING

1 ounce dried wood ear mushrooms

8 ounces ground pork

1 tablespoon fish sauce

¼ teaspoon salt

1 teaspoon freshly ground black pepper

2 tablespoons vegetable oil, plus more to grease the pan

2 tablespoons minced shallot

½ cup Crispy Fried Shallots, for topping (optional)

To make the sauce

In a large bowl, whisk the water, fish sauce, rice vinegar, and sugar until the sugar dissolves. Add fresh hot chile slices (if using). Set aside.

To make the batter

In a large bowl or saucepan, whisk the flour, water, and oil until combined. Set aside.

To make the filling

1. Soak the wood ear mushrooms in hot water for 10 minutes. Drain well. Squeeze out the excess water. Trim the roots, if any. Chop with a knife or use a food processor.
2. In a bowl, mix the pork, mushrooms, fish sauce, salt, and pepper.
3. Heat a sauté pan over high heat and swirl in the oil to spread it evenly. Add the shallot and stir-fry until fragrant, about 1 minute. Add the pork mixture and stir-fry until cooked through, about 5 minutes. Transfer to a bowl.

To make the crêpes

1. Prepare a dry, flat surface, like a wooden cutting board, and grease the surface with vegetable oil.
2. Heat a small nonstick sauté pan over medium heat. Drizzle in 1 teaspoon of oil, then wipe off the excess oil with a paper towel. Reduce the heat to low.

3. Stir the batter. Lift the pan off the flame and ladle about ¼ cup of the batter into the pan. Tilt the pan in a circular motion to spread the batter evenly and thinly. Return the pan to the stove and cover. Cook until the crêpe looks transparent, about 1 minute. Remove from the heat and tap the pan, upside down, against the greased cutting board so the crêpe falls out cleanly.

4. Spoon some filling one-third of the way down the end of the crêpe farthest from you. Start rolling. Once you get the hang of it, you can cook a new crêpe while you're rolling the previous one. Each time, give the batter a stir before ladling it into the pan. Lightly grease and wipe the pan again after about 5 crêpes.

5. Cut the rolls into pieces. Sprinkle with crispy fried shallots (if using) and serve with the sweet and sour fish sauce.

Ingredient tip: I use Vĩnh Thuận brand of bánh cuốn flour, which is available in Vietnamese stores and on Amazon. If you can't find bánh cuốn flour, mix 7 ounces rice starch with 7 ounces tapioca starch.

Crispy Savory Crêpes
Bánh Xèo

SERVES 4 • PREP TIME: 35 MINUTES • COOK TIME: 45 MINUTES

Bánh xèo is a popular street food and also an easy one to make at home. It's especially suitable for gatherings because it's highly customizable. I learned this dish from a southern friend of mine when I went to her bánh xèo party in New York a few years ago. You'll need an 8-inch nonstick sauté pan for this recipe.

FOR THE BATTER

1 (14.1-ounce) package bánh xèo flour (including the tiny packet of turmeric inside)

2 cups water

1 cup beer

½ cup coconut milk

5 scallions, chopped

FOR THE FILLING

8 ounces pork loin, shoulder, or belly, thinly sliced against the grain

1 pound large shrimp, peeled and deveined

1 teaspoon salt

1 teaspoon freshly ground black pepper

Vegetable oil, for cooking

1 cup bean sprouts

1 head lettuce

1 cup fresh mint leaves

1 cup fresh cilantro, perilla leaf, Vietnamese balm, or Thai/Asian basil leaves

4 recipes Sweet and Sour Fish Sauce Dip

To make the batter

In a bowl, whisk the flour, turmeric, water, beer, coconut milk, and scallion until combined. Cover and let sit for 30 minutes.

To make the filling and crêpes

1. In a bowl, combine the pork and shrimp and season with the salt and pepper.
2. Heat a medium sauté pan over high heat. Swirl in 1½ tablespoons of oil to spread it evenly. Add a few slices of pork and a few shrimp. Stir-fry until the pork and shrimp are cooked and nicely brown, about 4 minutes.
3. Stir the batter. Lift the pan off the flame and ladle about ⅓ cup of batter into the pan. Tilt the pan in a circular motion to spread the batter evenly and thinly. Return the pan to the stove and reduce the heat to low.
4. Add the bean sprouts. Drizzle 1 tablespoon of oil around the edge of the crêpe. Cover and cook for about 5 minutes. Fold the crêpe to form a semi-circle and remove from the pan.
5. Use scissors to cut the crêpe in half. Wrap each half in a lettuce leaf with some mint and cilantro. Repeat with the remaining filling and batter.
6. Serve the bánh xèo with the fish sauce dip.

Variation tip: The filling for bánh xèo is highly customizable. You can substitute shredded carrots for bean sprouts and add beef, seafood, and mushroom as well.

Substitution tip: I use Vĩnh Thuận brand bánh xèo flour, which is available in Vietnamese stores and on Amazon. If you can't find bánh xèo flour, mix 14 ounces rice flour with 1½ teaspoons ground turmeric and ¼ teaspoon salt.

Chicken Curry BáNH MÌ *Bánh Mì Cà-Ri Gà*

SERVES 3 • PREP TIME: 30 MINUTES • COOK TIME: 40 MINUTES

Curry, or cà-ri, as we Vietnamese call it, reflects the multicultural nature of the central and southern regions, both strongly influenced by India during the time of the Champa Kingdom. Vietnamese curry uses Indian curry powder and Thai (Siam) coconut, and is served with the Vietnamese bánh mì (French baguette). Vietnamese curry broth is lighter and thinner than Indian curry, and it usually contains three Vietnamese staples: lemongrass, taro, and herbs. Either light or dark chicken meat goes well with this recipe, with the curry making up for the drier flavor of the light meat.

1 pound boneless, skinless chicken thighs, cut into 1½-inch pieces

2 tablespoons curry powder, divided

Pinch salt

1½ teaspoons freshly ground black pepper

5 tablespoons vegetable oil, divided

2 yams (about 1 pound total), peeled and cut into 1½-inch pieces

1 taro root (about 10 ounces), peeled and cut into 1½-inch pieces

3 tablespoons minced garlic, divided

2 tablespoons minced ginger

10 lemongrass stalks

1 tablespoon minced hot chiles

¼ cup sugar

¼ cup soy sauce

2½ cups boiling water

½ cup coconut milk

1 cup fresh basil leaves, chopped

3 Vietnamese baguettes or Portuguese rolls, or 1 French baguette

1. In a bowl, season the chicken with 1 tablespoon of curry powder and the salt and pepper. Set aside.

2. Heat a sauté pan over high heat. Swirl in 3 tablespoons of oil to spread it evenly. Add the yam and taro and cook until lightly golden, about 3 minutes per side. Transfer the yam and taro to a plate.

3. Add 2 tablespoons of garlic and the ginger to the oil remaining in the pan and stir-fry for about 1 minute. Add the chicken and stir-fry for about 2 minutes. Remove the pan from the heat.

4. Bruise the lemongrass stalks with a pestle or a meat hammer to release the fragrance. Bunch them together and tie with a lemongrass leaf.

5. Heat the remaining 2 tablespoons of oil in a saucepan over medium heat. Add the remaining 1 tablespoon garlic and stir-fry for 1 minute. Add the fried yam and taro, chiles, sugar, remaining 1 tablespoon of curry powder, and soy sauce and mix lightly. Add the boiling water and the lemongrass bundle. Lower the heat to medium-low, cover, and cook until the yam and taro are soft, about 20 minutes.

6. Increase the heat to high. Stir in the chicken and cook for 5 minutes. Remove the pan from the heat and gently stir in the coconut milk and basil.

7. Heat a heavy skillet or sauté pan over high heat. Heat the baguettes for about 2 minutes on each side to make them crispy before serving.

8. Break the baguettes with your hands and dip them in the curry stew.

Substitution tip: You can substitute carrot for taro.

Variation tip: This dish can also be served over steamed rice.

Cooking tip: You might want to wear gloves when handling taro, because it can make your hands feel itchy. If this happens, prepare a bowl of warm water mixed with vinegar or lime juice. The heat and the acid will make the itch go away.

Storage tip: *The curry can be kept in the refrigerator for up to 3 days.*

Vegan Curry BáNh Mì

Bánh Mì Cà-Ri Ch

SERVES 2 • PREP TIME: 20 MINUTES • COOK TIME: 30 MINUTES

Every month, on the night of the full moon, all houses in the old town of Hội An, where I live, turn off their electric lights. The whole town is lit up by the moon, lanterns, and candles floating along the river. On that night, our favorite thing to do is go to our favorite cozy riverside restaurant and sample their amazing vegan menu. This recipe is inspired by my favorite curry dish there. You'll love the creamy and rich broth that's perfect with every bite of crispy baguette.

1 (10-ounce) block firm tofu

6 tablespoons vegetable oil, divided

2 yams (about 1 pound total), peeled and cut into 1½-inch pieces

1 taro root (about 10 ounces), peeled and cut into 1½-inch pieces

10 lemongrass stalks

3 tablespoons minced garlic

1 eggplant (pick the longer, thinner type), cut into 1½-inch pieces

1 tablespoon minced hot chiles

¼ cup soy sauce

¼ cup sugar

2 tablespoons curry powder

2½ cups boiling water

½ cup coconut milk

1 cup fresh basil leaves, coarsely chopped

3 Vietnamese baguettes or Portuguese rolls, or 1 French baguette

1. Pat the tofu dry with a paper towel, the drier, the better to reduce spattering when frying. Halve the tofu lengthwise and then cut it crosswise into 8 pieces.

2. Heat a medium sauté pan over medium-high heat. Swirl in 4 tablespoons of oil to spread it evenly. Add the tofu, and fry until golden on the bottom, about 7 minutes. Flip over and fry the other side until golden, about 5 minutes. Transfer the tofu to a plate.

3. Add the yam and taro to the pan and fry until lightly golden, about 4 minutes on each side. Transfer the yam and taro to the plate with the tofu.

4. Bruise the lemongrass stalks with a pestle or a meat hammer to release the fragrance. Bunch them together and tie with a lemongrass leaf.

5. Heat the remaining 2 tablespoons of oil in a saucepan over medium heat. Add the garlic and stir-fry for 1 minute. Add the fried yam, taro, tofu, eggplant, and chiles. Add the soy sauce, sugar, and curry powder and lightly mix. Add the boiling water and the lemongrass bundle. Lower the heat to medium-low, cover, and cook until the yam and taro are soft, about 20 minutes.

6. Remove the pan from the heat and gently stir in the coconut milk and chopped basil.

7. Heat a heavy skillet or sauté pan over high heat. Heat the baguettes for about 2 minutes on each side to make them crispy before serving.

8. Break the baguettes and dip them in the curry stew.

Variation tip: This vegan curry can be served over steamed rice.

Ingredient tip: Buy Japanese or Korean yams if possible because they're sweeter and more flavorful than other types.

Storage tip: The curry can be kept in the refrigerator for up to 3 days.

Baguette With Beef in Red Wine Stew *Bánh Mì Bò Sốt Vang*

SERVES 2 • PREP TIME: 20 MINUTES • COOK TIME: 1 HOUR

Bò sốt vang combines classic French cooking with the Vietnamese love of topping our food with fresh-cut herbs. This creates a mix of tastes alternating between savory and aromatic, reaching both the tongue and the nose. Despite its simplicity, this soup is one I'm sure you'll want to come back to again and again, since the flavor only gets better after two or three days!

1 pound boneless ribeye steak or beef shank, cut into 1-inch cubes

2 tablespoons minced garlic, divided

2 cups red wine, divided

2 tablespoons salt, divided

1 teaspoon freshly ground black pepper

1 tablespoon five-spice powder or ground cinnamon

8 tablespoons (1 stick) unsalted butter, divided

2 cups finely chopped onion

2 cups finely chopped tomato

1 small carrot (optional), diced

½ cup fresh cilantro leaves, coarsely chopped

2 Vietnamese baguettes or Portuguese rolls, or 1 French baguette

1. In a bowl, toss the beef with 1 tablespoon of garlic, 2 tablespoons of red wine, 1 tablespoon of salt, the pepper, and five-spice powder. Set aside.

2. In a saucepan over high heat, melt 4 tablespoons of butter. Add the onion and stir-fry for about 2 minutes. Add the tomato and remaining 1 tablespoon of

salt. Stir-fry until the onion and tomato are soft and become a paste, about 3 minutes.

3. Meanwhile, in a sauté pan over high heat, melt the remaining 4 tablespoons of butter. Add the remaining 1 tablespoon of garlic and stir until fragrant, about 1 minute. Add the beef and stir constantly until brown, 1 to 2 minutes.

4. Transfer the beef to the pan with the onion and tomato. Add the carrot (if using) and the remaining red wine. Stir well and bring to a boil over medium-high heat. Stir again to make sure nothing is sticking to the bottom of the pan. Reduce the heat to low, cover, and cook until the beef and carrot are soft, about 1 hour. Scatter the cilantro over the top.

5. Heat a heavy skillet or sauté pan over high heat. Heat the baguettes for about 2 minutes on each side to make them crispy before serving.

6. Break the baguettes and dip them in the stew.

Cooking tip: *Some Vietnamese like to make this stew thicker by adding a slurry of 1 tablespoon cornstarch whisked into 2 tablespoons water. At the end of the cooking time, turn the heat to medium-high and stir in the slurry. Cook for about 2 more minutes until the stew thickens. Serve.*

Storage tip: *You can keep this stew in the refrigerator for 3 days.*

Bánh Mì Fillings

Although bánh mì fillings vary from cart to cart and from city to city, the popular ones include mayonnaise, pickles, chili sauce, and pâté. Mayonnaise is always fresh-made, never from a jar, and it helps bind ingredients and add a creamy texture. In contrast, homemade Vietnamese pickled vegetables add sweet and sour flavors to balance the tastes of fat and protein. I recommend purchasing the pâté and chili sauce; however, if you would like to make fillings at home, by all means do make the mayonnaise and pickles yourself so you can enjoy the fresh tastes that are so much better than pre-made. Mayonnaise, pickles, chili, pâté, cilantro, and an omelet or ham are all you need for a simple, classic, delicious bánh mì.

Homemade Mayonnaise *Sốt Mai-ô-ne*

MAKES **2/3** CUP • PREP TIME: 10 MINUTES

I learned how to make mayonnaise from my friend Sơn Trần, a European-trained chef who runs two restaurants in Vietnam. He takes food very seriously, not because of his restaurants, but because of the great joy he finds in making everything from scratch, including fish sauce and soy sauce. He once even chopped down a mango tree in his garden to get the kind of wood he wanted to smoke his own salmon with. I helped him videotape a tutorial on how to make mayonnaise, and I was amazed at the simplicity and beauty. Since that time, I've never wanted dismal store-bought mayonnaise again!

3 large egg yolks

Juice of 1 lime wedge

Pinch salt

½ cup plus 1 tablespoon vegetable oil or extra-virgin olive oil

In a bowl, whisk together the egg yolks, lime juice, and salt. Continue whisking, adding the oil in a slow, steady stream, until the mixture becomes creamy, smooth, and thick, about 5 minutes.

> ***Cooking tip:*** *You can also use a hand mixer to whisk the mixture.*
>
> ***Storage tip:*** *Keep the mayonnaise in a glass jar in the refrigerator for up to 5 days.*

Carrot and Daikon Pickles *Đồ Chua*

MAKES 1 QUART • PREP TIME: 30 MINUTES

These carrot and daikon pickles are ubiquitous in Vietnam, popular in baguette fillings as well as vermicelli salad bowls. We believe that they help with digestion, and their fresh flavors are a great accompaniment to protein-rich foods. Don't worry if you're not a fan of deli-style dill pickles because these don't taste like that; rather, they taste like fresh salad tossed in a perfect dressing. These pickles can be kept in the refrigerator for a month, but my family and I usually kill the whole jar within a day.

3 small carrots (about 10 ounces total), peeled and shredded

3 small daikon (about 1½ pounds total), peeled and shredded

2 tablespoons salt

1 cup rice vinegar

½ cup water

½ cup sugar

1. In a mixing bowl, toss together the carrots, daikon, and salt. Let sit for 10 minutes.

2. Meanwhile, in another bowl, whisk the vinegar, water, and sugar until the sugar dissolves. This is your brine.

3. Rinse the carrots and daikon under running water, then drain well. Squeeze them with your hands or with a cheesecloth to keep the pickles crunchy and allow them to absorb the brine more quickly.

4. Transfer the carrots and daikon to a quart-size jar. Cover with the brine. Cover the jar and refrigerate for at least 4 hours before serving.

Substitution tip: *For baguette filling, if you don't have time to make pickles, thin cucumber slices will do.*

Variation tip: *Add fresh hot chile slices to the jar if you like it spicy.*

Grilled Pork Bánh Mì
Bánh Mì o Nướng

SERVES 3 • PREP TIME: 30 MINUTES + 1 HOUR TO MARINATE • COOK TIME: 20 MINUTES

Believe it or not, the best grilled pork bánh mì I've ever had was at a food fair in Pittsburgh, when my husband and I were taking a road trip just before moving back to Vietnam. It was delicious, but what made it even more memorable was that the vendor, a nice older Vietnamese woman, gave us a free one after hearing my husband speak in his rudimentary Vietnamese.

If you have space and the weather is nice, of course it's best to grill your pork outside in order to get that special smoky taste. However, don't fret if you don't have a grill: Pan-grilling is quicker and more convenient for many home cooks.

FOR THE GRILLED PORK

1 pound pork shoulder, thinly sliced against the grain

1 tablespoon minced shallot

1 tablespoon minced garlic

3 tablespoons fish sauce

2 tablespoons honey

2 tablespoons light sesame oil, divided

1 tablespoon five-spice powder or ground cinnamon

¼ teaspoon salt

1 teaspoon freshly ground black pepper

FOR THE BÁNH MÌ

3 Vietnamese baguettes or Portuguese rolls, or 1 French baguette, cut into thirds

3 tablespoons Homemade Mayonnaise

Chili sauce or fresh hot chile slices (optional)

1 cup Carrot and Daikon Pickles or cucumber slices

½ cup fresh cilantro leaves

½ cup fresh mint leaves

To make the grilled pork

1. In a bowl, combine the pork, shallot, garlic, fish sauce, honey, 1 tablespoon of oil, five-spice powder, salt, and pepper. Mix well and let marinate for at least 1 hour at room temperature or as long as overnight, covered, in the refrigerator.
2. Heat a sauté pan over high heat. Swirl in the remaining 1 tablespoon of oil to spread it evenly. When you see a little smoke coming off the pan, add the pork. Fry until one side is golden, 1 to 2 minutes. Flip and fry until the other side is golden, about 1 more minute. Turn off the heat and let the pork sit in the pan.

To assemble the bánh mì

1. Slice the baguettes lengthwise almost all the way through. Close them back up again and heat them in a hot sauté pan or in the oven briefly to crisp the outsides.
2. Spread the cut sides with mayonnaise and chili sauce (if using). Add the pickles and hot chiles (if using), then the pork. Top with cilantro and mint and serve.

> ***Variation tip:*** *Besides being popular baguette fillings, grilled pork is a classic addition to serve with rice vermicelli. To assemble, toss together rice vermicelli with the pork, pickles, and herbs. Top with roasted peanuts and drizzle with Sweet and Sour Fish Sauce Dip.*
>
> ***Cooking tip:*** *You can also roast the pork in the oven. Preheat the oven to 450°F. Line a baking sheet with aluminum foil. Grease the foil and spread out the pork slices. Bake until cooked through, 15 to 20 minutes, then turn on the broiler and broil for 3 minutes.*

Grilled Chicken Bánh Mì

Bánh Mì Gà Nướng

SERVES 3 • PREP TIME: 20 MINUTES + 1 HOUR TO MARINATE • COOK TIME: 20 MINUTES

While grilled pork filling has been around for a long time, I only had my first bánh mì with chicken filling a few years ago in New York. Now back in Vietnam, I've noticed that bánh mì vendors here in the central region also usually offer a grilled chicken option. I have a feeling that option is more to suit Western tourists' taste preference, but I'm happy they do it, because Vietnamese lemongrass chicken is something you can't miss. Of course, you'll have to visit Vietnam for the best chickens in the world, but you can get pretty close using this recipe! For this recipe, my Vietnamese mouth and tummy always prefer chicken thigh meat, but you can use any part of the chicken you like.

FOR THE GRILLED CHICKEN

1 pound boneless, skinless chicken thighs, cut into 1-inch chunks

2 tablespoons minced lemongrass

2 tablespoons minced ginger

3 tablespoons fish sauce

3 tablespoons light sesame oil, divided

1 tablespoon honey

FOR THE BÁNH MÌ

3 Vietnamese baguettes or Portuguese rolls, or 1 French baguette, cut into thirds

1 cup Carrot and Daikon Pickles or cucumber slices

3 tablespoons Homemade Mayonnaise

Chili sauce or fresh hot chile slices (optional)

½ cup fresh cilantro leaves

½ cup fresh mint leaves

To make the chicken

1. In a bowl, mix the chicken, lemongrass, ginger, fish sauce, 2 tablespoons of oil, and the honey. Mix well and set aside to marinate for 1 hour.
2. Preheat the oven to 450°F.
3. Line a baking sheet with aluminum foil. Grease the foil with the remaining 1 tablespoon of oil, then spread out the chicken in a single layer. Bake for 20 minutes.

To assemble the bánh mì

1. Slice the baguettes lengthwise almost all the way through. Close them back up again and heat them in a hot sauté pan or in the oven briefly to crisp the outsides.
2. Spread the cut sides with mayonnaise and chili sauce (if using). Add the pickles and hot chiles (if using), then the chicken. Top with cilantro and mint and serve.

Substitution tip: Chicken can be changed out for shrimp in this recipe.

Variation tip: This dish can also be served over steamed rice or rice vermicelli with herbs and Sweet and Sour Fish Sauce Dip.

Pineapple Shrimp Bánh Mì *Bánh Mì Kẹp Tôm*

SERVES 3 • PREP TIME: 10 MINUTES • COOK TIME: 15 MINUTES

I learned this modern recipe from my favorite restaurant in historic Hội An. Pineapple and seafood are a typical combination in this region of Vietnam. The pineapple sauce in this dish gives the baguette a refreshing flavor. It's also quick and easy to make. You don't need pickles, mayonnaise, or chili sauce here because the shrimp and pineapple naturally balance out the sweet, sour, salty, and spicy flavors.

FOR THE SHRIMP

1 pound large shrimp, peeled and deveined

2 tablespoons minced shallot, divided

2 tablespoons fish sauce

1 teaspoon freshly ground black pepper

½ teaspoon sugar

4 tablespoons vegetable oil, divided

1 tablespoon minced garlic

1 cup finely chopped pineapple

1 tablespoon minced fresh hot chile

1 teaspoon salt

FOR THE BÁNH MÌ

3 Vietnamese baguettes or Portuguese rolls, or 1 French baguette, cut into thirds

½ cup fresh cilantro leaves

½ cup fresh mint leaves

To make the shrimp

1. In a bowl, toss together the shrimp, 1 tablespoon of shallots, the fish sauce, pepper, and sugar. Set aside.

2. Heat a medium sauté pan over high heat. Swirl in 2 tablespoons of oil. Add the garlic and stir-fry until fragrant, about 1 minute. Reduce the heat to medium. Add the pineapple, hot chile, and salt. Stir-fry for about 2 minutes.

3. In a medium saucepan, heat the remaining 2 tablespoons of oil over medium-high heat. Add the remaining 1 tablespoon of shallots. Stir-fry until fragrant, about 1 minute. Reduce the heat to medium. Add the shrimp and stir-fry until the shrimp starts to brown, about 5 minutes. Stir in the pineapple mixture. Cook for about 3 more minutes, stirring occasionally so the pineapple sauce coats the shrimp evenly. Remove the pan from the heat.

To assemble the bánh mì

4. Slice the baguettes lengthwise almost all the way through. Close them again and heat briefly in a hot sauté pan or oven to crisp the outsides.

5. Spread the cut sides with some of the pineapple sauce. Add the shrimp, mint, and cilantro and serve.

Variation tip: This dish can be served over steamed rice.

Vietnam's Best Bánh Mì

In my opinion, the old town of Hội An, where I live now, has the best bánh mì in the country. You can watch Anthony Bourdain's Vietnam episode to learn more about the magical flavors they put into the baguettes here. One of the most popular fillings in bánh mì carts here is char siu meat; Hội An people call it siu meat for short. In Cantonese, siu means "burn" or, in this context, "roast," and while traditionally this is a roasted dish, people here have adjusted the cooking method to slow-cooking in a sauté pan. The result is tender, well-marinated meat with a rich, aromatic sauce that adds layers of flavors to local noodle dishes and baguettes.

Char Siu Pork Bánh Mì

Bánh Mì Thit Xá Xíu

SERVES 3 • PREP TIME: 15 MINUTES + 20 MINUTES TO MARINATE • COOK TIME: 30 MINUTES

I never cared much about making char siu pork at home until my neighbor gave me a big plate of it to thank me and I suddenly became aware of how delicious homemade char siu pork could be. This is my neighbor's recipe, passed down from her mother and grandmother. Central Vietnamese char siu pork is different from the original Cantonese version. We use a braising method instead of grilling to make the most of the sauce for baguettes. Also, lemongrass is used instead of fermented bean curd, which adds a tropical aroma.

FOR THE CHAR SIU

2 tablespoons soy sauce

1 tablespoon five-spice powder

1 tablespoon sugar

1 teaspoon freshly ground black pepper

¼ teaspoon salt

3 tablespoons minced garlic, divided

2 tablespoons minced lemongrass, divided

10 ounces pork shoulder or belly, cut into 1-inch chunks

2 tablespoons vegetable oil

½ cup boiling water

FOR THE BÁNH MÌ

3 Vietnamese baguettes or Portuguese rolls, or 1 French baguette, cut into thirds

3 tablespoons Homemade Mayonnaise

Chili sauce or fresh hot chile slices (optional)

1 cup Carrot and Daikon Pickles or cucumber slices

½ cup fresh cilantro leaves

½ cup fresh mint leaves

To make the char siu

1. In a bowl, whisk the soy sauce, five-spice powder, sugar, salt, and pepper until the sugar dissolves. Add 1 tablespoon of garlic and 1 tablespoon of lemongrass and mix well. Add the pork and rub the soy sauce mixture into it. Set aside to marinate for 30 minutes.

2. Heat a sauté pan or saucepan over high heat. Swirl in the oil to spread it evenly. Add the pork and cook until brown, about 4 minutes on each side. Add the remaining 2 tablespoons of garlic and the remaining 1 tablespoon of lemongrass, and stir-fry for about 1 minute to release the fragrance.

3. Reduce the heat to low. Add the boiling water. Cook, turning the meat occasionally, until the meat is honey-brown and the sauce is reduced by half, 20 to 25 minutes.

To assemble the bánh mì

1. Slice the baguettes lengthwise almost all the way through. Close them back up again and heat them in a hot sauté pan or in the oven.

2. Spread the cut sides with mayonnaise and chili sauce (if using). Add pickles and chile slices (if using), then the pork. Top with cilantro and mint and serve.

> *Variation tip:* You can serve this dish with steamed rice or rice vermicelli as well. If you use vermicelli, make sure to add some fresh mint, cilantro, and/or basil.

Chicken Phở

Chapter Five

Phở
NOODLE SOUP

Classic Phở   *Phở Bò*

Beef Meatballs   *Bò Viên*

Stir-Fried Beef Phở   *Phở Xào*

Chicken Phở   *Phở Gà*

Chicken Phở Salad   *Phở Gà Trộn*

Beef Phở Rolls   *Phở Cuốn*

Red Wine Beef Stew Phở   *Phở Sốt Vang*

Unlike most traditional Vietnamese dishes created by rice-growing farmers in the countryside, phở is a relatively modern urban creation that originated in the city of Hanoi and only reached rural parts of the country in recent decades. Learning about the origins of a bowl of phở is like reviewing the most eventful century in Vietnamese history.

This pure Hanoi delicacy came to life in the early 20th century in times of interesting and tumultuous multicultural undercurrents. In an attempt to facilitate trade between Tonkin (North Vietnam) and China, French colonists allowed a new wave of Chinese immigrants into Tonkin. This area soon became a cultural melting pot where various languages were spoken. Many modern researchers try to explain the origins of the name phở by pointing to a phonetic similarity between French *pot-au-feu* and Cantonese *rou fen*.

Regardless of the name's mysterious origin, it was "phở sure" the French who indirectly propelled phở into stardom. Prior to the French colonial period, the Vietnamese didn't eat beef because cows were needed to plow fields and pull carriages. In the early twentieth century, there were only a few beef butchers in Hanoi, mainly to supply meat to the French. In his research collection about Hanoi in the twentieth century, Vietnamese writer Siêu Hải explained how phở, an internationally known beef soup, came about from a nation whose people found eating beef an alien idea. He suggested that phở originated from a Vietnamese dish called xáo trâu, which was popular among Vietnamese workers in the marketplace. Xáo trâu consisted of slices of water buffalo meat, herbs, and broth over bún (round, thin rice noodles). After selling the best meat to the French, beef butchers often sold the unwanted bones and remnants, from which xáo trâu vendors created a beef variation called xáo bò. Later, they realized that the sour taste of the bun noodle, made from fermented rice, didn't really match the flavor of beef and beef broth in their new food creation. They replaced the bún with a new invention inspired by another popular traditional dish—bánh cuốn, or plain steamed rice crêpe rolls. They made the crêpes thicker and cut them into flat strips, which is how the phở noodle has been made ever since.

Some foreigners think that phở is the name of the noodle, but phở means the whole dish, and the noodle is bánh phở, meaning starch-based food for phở. Bánh phở is widely available in Hanoi markets as both whole crêpes and cut strips. When I was small, phở sellers used to cut crêpes into noodles using a cleaver, something that was fun to watch while eating. Today, phở noodles are cut by the noodle makers before being delivered to phở vendors.

Phở began to spread from northern cities after the Geneva Agreements of 1954, when Vietnam was split in half and almost a million northerners, bringing Chinese cultural influences, migrated south. In the southern version, the noodles are not northern bánh phở, but rather more like hủ tiếu, a Cantonese noodle popular in Saigon. Southerners eat the dish with Chinese hoisin sauce and red chili sauce, along with a generous serving of blanched bean sprouts. Rock sugar is also added to the stock, creating a sweet flavor distinctive of southern food. Because the Vietnamese who arrived in the United States after 1975 were mainly from the south, the phở that has made its way to American tables is primarily a southern version.

Today, classic phở in northern Vietnam remains the same. Besides classic phở, variations like phở xào (stir-fried beef phở), phở cuốn (beef phở rolls), and phở trộn (phở salad) have survived Hanoians' picky tastes since the mid-twentieth century until now. A rule of thumb in the North is to pick a vendor that sells only one type of phở. A place that sells both chicken and beef phở, or sells both phở soup and phở salad, is usually a bad sign. A phở vendor must specialize in one aspect of their craft or risk being mediocre at all of them.

PhO in Literature

Phở quickly became a popular street food in Hanoi. Prominent Hanoi-based contemporary writers like Thạch Lam, Nguyễn Tuân, and Vũ Bằng describe phở in their literary works as one of the city's signature street foods. They agree that phở is a pure, delicate treat, perfect for both early breakfast and late-night supper. Classic phở consists of bánh phở, beef, scallion, cilantro, hot chile slices, and a wedge of lime or chili vinegar. However, the soul of phở is the broth. It has to be clear but rich, fine but flavorful, and, most importantly, it has to be an honest umami broth, meaning no sugar added. In his critically acclaimed 1957 book, Delicious Bites of Hanoi, *Vũ Bằng calls adding sugar to phở broth "a clumsy act," arguing that eating phở broth seasoned with sugar is a waste of money as well as a waste of time and effort spent on eating. It is, as he puts it, "a true frustration."*

Classic Pho *Phở Bò*

MAKES 4 BOWLS • PREP TIME: 15 MINUTES + 1 HOUR TO SOAK • COOK TIME: 4 HOURS

Cooking phở or making the stock is quite straightforward. The cook simmers bones and meat with ginger, onion, and dry spices. Beef bones take a long time to release their flavors, but it's mostly just simmering time. Ginger, shallots, and onions must be charred (you can do this directly over your stove's gas flame), and dry spices must be roasted in a pan before being added to the broth. It may sound complicated, but it takes just minutes to prepare. Once you throw all the ingredients in the stockpot, you can take a nap or watch a movie or two while letting the stove do the work.

2½ tablespoons salt, divided

4 (2-inch) pieces ginger, 2 lightly smashed and 2 left whole

2½ pounds beef marrow bones

1½ pound beef shank or brisket

5 shallots or 2 onions

2 star anise

1 black cardamom pod

1 (2-inch) cinnamon stick

¼ cup fish sauce

14 ounces dry phở noodles, cooked according to package instructions (or see here)

1 pound beef tenderloin, also known as filet mignon, thinly sliced against the grain (optional)

8 scallions, white parts halved lengthwise and green parts chopped

1 cup fresh cilantro leaves or Thai/Asian basil leaves, coarsely chopped

1 lime, cut into wedges, for serving

Fresh hot chile slices or hot chili sauce, for serving (optional)

Freshly ground black pepper, for serving

1. Fill a large stockpot with water and add 2 tablespoons of salt and the smashed ginger. Add the bones and beef shank and soak for 1 to 2 hours. Drain. Return the bones and beef shank to the pot.

2. Pour in enough fresh water to cover the bones and beef shank. Bring to a boil over high heat. Drain. Rinse the bones and beef shank and return them to the pot.

3. Char the whole ginger pieces and shallots by poking with a fork and grilling over a gas flame. Rinse under running water to cool. Peel the black skin lightly to release the fragrance. Add them to the stockpot with the bones and beef shank.

4. Heat a sauté pan over high heat. Stir-fry the star anise, black cardamom, and cinnamon stick until fragrant, 1 to 2 minutes. Be careful not to burn them. Secure them in a tea ball or tea bag and add it to the stockpot.

5. Add 8 cups of fresh water to the stockpot and bring to a boil over high heat. Reduce the heat to low, cover, and simmer for 1 hour. Remove the beef shank from the pot and set aside to cool. Continue to simmer the stock, covered, for 1 more hour and then remove the tea ball of spices. Cover and simmer for 2 hours. Season with the remaining ½ tablespoon of salt and the fish sauce.

6. Thinly slice the beef shank.

7. If desired, rinse four bowls with boiling water. Blanch the phở noodles in boiling water for 1 minute. (These steps will keep the phở bowls hot and are optional.)

8. Distribute the phở noodles among the bowls. Add the beef shank. Scatter the raw tenderloin slices evenly over the noodles, if using. Add the scallions. Ladle boiling stock into each bowl. Start pouring over the raw meat first so the boiling stock cooks the raw meat right away. There should be enough stock to cover the meat and noodles in each bowl.

9. Scatter the chopped herbs over each bowl. Serve immediately with lime wedges, chile slices or chili sauce (if using), and pepper on the side.

Substitution tip: *Black cardamom pods, star anise, and cinnamon sticks are available in most supermarkets or on Amazon. You can also buy a small pre-packaged phở spice bag, which consists of the previously mentioned spices plus whole cloves, coriander seeds, and fennel seeds. However, I usually leave out these three items, because they make the phở broth a little stronger than the northern style I'm used to.*

Ingredient tip: *Freeze the filet mignon for 30 to 45 minutes to make it easier to slice thinly.*

Cooking tip: *After simmering the stock for hours, there will be a pale yellow layer of fat on top. It's personal preference to keep it or not. I like it because fat from marrow bones is tasty, but others prefer their broth clear and clean. If you want to remove the fat on the surface, uncover and increase the heat to high. The fat will float to the edge of the pot. Skim the fat using a fine-mesh skimmer. Alternatively, let the stock cool down in the refrigerator for 2 hours or overnight. The fat will rise to the top, harden, and be very easy to remove. Bring the stock to a boil before serving.*

Storage tip: *Store boiled phở noodles and boiled beef slices in the refrigerator for up to 5 days. Blanch the beef in a pot of boiling water for 1 minute. Blanch the phở noodles in a pot of boiling water for 2 minutes and drain well before serving.*

How To Eat PhO

Phở is not a food for social gatherings and chitchat; it's supposed to be finished as quickly as possible before it gets cool. We often joke that if somebody looks sweaty, as if they have just come out of the sauna, then that person has eaten phở the right way. When eating phở, we always start with a spoon of broth first to see if it's balanced, then we decide if we need to add a little bit of lime juice or not. Some renowned phở places whose owners are proud of their broth quality don't even offer lime or side condiments. They believe their bowls of phở are perfect just the way they are, and believe that one tiny addition of any condiments can ruin their elegant broth. If you have ever worked on a broth for 6 to 10 hours, you can understand their pride!

Beef Meatballs *Bò Viên*

MAKES ABOUT 12 MEATBALLS • PREP TIME: 10 MINUTES + 6 HOURS TO CHILL • COOK TIME: 15 MINUTES

Southern open-mindedness and multicultural influence have made phở toppings more diverse, with the addition of beef meatballs and sometimes exotic parts like tripe, tail chunks, and tendon. Beef meatballs are another Cantonese influence on southern phở. These can be served as the only meat topping or as add-ons to classic beef slices in a phở bowl.

Good meatballs taste like premium German sausage, with a fine but bouncy texture. The secret is to mince the beef very finely while keeping it cold the whole time. The traditional way is to pound the meat with a heavy granite or stone mortar and pestle, but a stand mixer or food processor will save you time and sweat.

1 pound beef shank, cut into ½-inch cubes

1 tablespoon fish sauce

1 teaspoon potato starch, cornstarch, or tapioca starch

¼ teaspoon baking soda

2 tablespoons ice water

1 tablespoon minced garlic

1 teaspoon freshly ground black pepper

Vegetable oil, for greasing the plate

Pinch salt

1. Put the beef cubes in a zip-top bag. Flatten the bag to spread out the meat cubes inside, seal, and freeze for 2 hours.
2. In a small bowl, mix the fish sauce, starch, and baking soda.

3. Transfer the chilled meat to a food processor. Add the fish sauce mixture and the ice water. Grind 5 times at the highest speed, each time for about 15 seconds. Pause for a few seconds after each round to prevent the food processor from getting too hot. After two or three rounds, scrape the meat off the sides of the bowl. Transfer the ground meat to a zip-top bag. Flatten the meat in the bag, seal, and put it in the freezer for 2 more hours. (If your food processor is small, divide the meat into two batches. Process one batch at a time while keeping the other in the freezer. Put the first batch back in the freezer before starting on the second batch.)

4. After the two hours, break the meat up with your hands and repeat the grinding process. Put the meat back in a zip-top bag, flatten, and freeze for 2 more hours.

5. Repeat the grinding process a third time but this time, add the garlic and pepper before grinding. The meat should be a fine, sticky, smooth, pale pink paste. Transfer the paste to a zip-top bag. Squeeze out the air and seal. Hit the bag against the ground 20 times. Alternatively, if you have a stand mixer, you can use the paddle attachment to beat the paste at low speed for 2 minutes, then increase the speed to medium and beat for 3 minutes.

6. Brush a plate with vegetable oil and wet your hands with water. Use a spoon to scoop the paste into your hand. Shape it into a ball about 1¼ inches in diameter and place it on the plate. Repeat with the remaining meat.

7. Fill a large bowl with ice water. Transfer the meatballs to a saucepan and add enough water to cover the meatballs, plus a pinch of salt. Bring to a boil over high heat, then reduce the heat to medium-low. Cover and cook for 10 minutes, swirling the meatballs around after 5 minutes. The meatballs should float when done. Take one out and rinse under running water to cool. Cut in half to check for doneness. If it's no longer pink in the middle, then the meat is done. Transfer the meatballs to the bowl of ice water. Let the meatballs cool, then drain well.

8. If desired, cut each ball in half before adding to phở. You can also cook the beef meatballs in phở stock and arrange a phở bowl as in the Classic Phở recipe.

Cooking tip: *If your butcher will grind your meat finely three times, you can skip the grinding process at home. Then just mix the ground meat with the fish sauce mixture and freeze for 2 hours. Break into small chunks and beat in the mixer for 2 minutes at low speed and then for 10 minutes at medium speed. You can also skip the step of beating the meat in the mixer or on the ground—the meatballs will have a softer, less bouncy texture but will still be very flavorful.*

Variation tip: *These are good with rice vermicelli and vegetable soup, or just on their own.*

Storage tip: *These meatballs can be frozen for up to 3 months. Defrost and cook in boiling water for about 5 minutes to reheat.*

Stir-Fried Beef Pho *Phở Xào*

SERVES 2 OR 3 • PREP TIME: 15 MINUTES • COOK TIME: 15 MINUTES

Phở xào uses stir-fried beef and vegetables on top of stir-fried phở noodles, with no broth. Phở xào came about after classic phở, and has been around in Hanoi for more than 50 years. When I was in college, there was a phở xào vendor across the street from my apartment. During finals, my roommate and I would go there around midnight to satisfy our hunger. Since phở xào is more expensive than regular phở, we could afford only one plate to share, but that only made the dish even more desirable and delicious.

8 ounces beef tenderloin or flank steak, thinly sliced against the grain

1 tablespoon soy sauce

1½ teaspoons freshly ground black pepper, plus more if necessary

5½ tablespoons vegetable oil, divided

3 tablespoons minced garlic, divided

1 pound yu choy or bok choy, cut into 2-inch strips

1 small carrot, thinly sliced (optional)

1 teaspoon salt

10 ounces dry phở noodles, cooked according to package instructions (or see here)

1 tablespoon fish sauce, plus more if necessary

1. In a bowl, season the beef with the soy sauce, pepper, and ½ tablespoon of oil. Set aside to marinate while you prepare the vegetables.

2. Heat a large sauté pan over high heat for 2 minutes. Swirl in 2 tablespoons of oil to spread it evenly. Add 1 tablespoon of garlic and stir-fry for 30 seconds. Add

the yu choy and carrot (if using) and stir-fry for 1 minute. Add the salt and stir-fry for 1 more minute. Transfer the vegetables to a large bowl.

3. Heat the same pan over high heat for 1 minute. Swirl in 1 tablespoon of oil to spread it evenly. Add 1 tablespoon of garlic and stir-fry for 30 seconds. Add the beef and stir-fry until almost brown, about 1 minute. Transfer the beef to the vegetable bowl.

4. Heat the same pan over high heat for 1 minute. Swirl in the remaining 2 tablespoons of oil to spread it evenly. Add the remaining 1 tablespoon of garlic and stir-fry for 30 seconds. Add the phở noodles. Try to break up any chunks and distribute the noodles evenly. Add the fish sauce and any juices that have accumulated in the beef and vegetable bowl. Stir-fry for 5 minutes. Add the beef and vegetables and stir-fry for 2 minutes.

5. Season with more fish sauce and black pepper. Mix well and serve immediately.

Substitution tip: *Instead of yu choy or bok choy, you can use a mixture of chopped celery and leek.*

Chicken Pho *Phở Gà*

SERVES 6 • PREP TIME: 10 MINUTES • COOK TIME: 40 MINUTES

At first, phở chicken was not welcomed by beef phở lovers. They said chicken stock and meat was bland compared to the rich beef bone stock. However, it soon became a favorite for its light and clean flavors. Chicken for phở in Vietnam has always been free range, not only because free-range chicken is widely available, but also because Vietnamese people prefer dark, firm meat.

Chicken phở reminds me of my boarding school days. I used to have chicken phở on the first day of each month when my parents gave me my allowance. I usually killed two bowls of chicken phở quite rapidly, enjoying my short-lived financial solvency.

1 (3-pound) chicken

3 quarts water

1 tablespoon salt, plus a pinch, divided

3 shallots

4 (2-inch) pieces ginger

1 onion, halved

¼ cup fish sauce, plus more if necessary

1 pound dry phở noodles, cooked according to package instructions (or see here)

6 scallions, white parts halved lengthwise and green parts chopped

2 cups fresh cilantro leaves, coarsely chopped

1 lime, cut into 6 wedges

Freshly ground black pepper

Hot chili sauce or fresh hot chile slices

1. Place the chicken, breast-side up, in a large stockpot. Add the water (it should cover the chicken) and a pinch of salt. Bring to a boil over medium heat. Reduce the heat to medium-low and cook for about 20 minutes. Check for doneness by poking a chopstick through the chicken thigh. If the juice runs clear, the meat is done. If it's still pink, cook for another 5 to 10 minutes.

2. Remove the chicken from the stock and let cool. When it cools down enough to handle, bone the chicken and return the bones to the stock. When the meat is completely cool, coarsely shred it. (Keep or discard the chicken skin to your preference.) Set aside.

3. Grill the shallots and ginger over a gas flame until they're charred. Rinse them under running water. Peel off the black skin and lightly smash to release their fragrance. Add the ginger, shallots, and onion to the stockpot. Cook over low heat for 30 minutes. Season with 1 tablespoon of salt. Turn off the heat. Add the fish sauce and stir well.

4. Distribute the phở noodles among bowls, then add the chicken and scallions. Ladle in the hot stock to cover the noodles and meat. Scatter the cilantro over the top and serve. Before eating, squeeze a wedge of lime juice into the bowl, sprinkle with pepper, and season with hot chili sauce or fresh chiles.

Chicken Phở Salad — *Phở Gà Trộn*

SERVES 2 • PREP TIME: 10 MINUTES • COOK TIME: 30 MINUTES

There are many chicken phở salad vendors in Hanoi, but the best known is a tiny vendor on a sidewalk of the Old Quarter. That place sells only in the evening and runs out very quickly. The sidewalk around that vendor is always packed with rows and rows of people waiting on scooters. When I was living in Hanoi, I often tried to get there early for a bowl of phở đùi (drumstick phở) because that dish sold out the fastest. Chicken phở salad is a nice change from chicken phở soup, with its delightful combination of fresh herbs, cold phở noodles, and chicken topped with sweet and sour soy sauce.

- 8 ounces chicken drumsticks
- 1 (2-inch) piece ginger, lightly smashed
- 1 teaspoon salt
- 3 tablespoons soy sauce
- 3 tablespoons rice vinegar
- 2½ tablespoons sugar
- 1½ tablespoons vegetable oil (optional)
- 1 tablespoon minced shallot
- 7 ounces dry phở noodles, cooked according to package instructions (or see here)
- 1 cup fresh cilantro leaves, coarsely chopped
- 1 cup fresh mint or Thai/Asian basil leaves, coarsely chopped
- Hot chili sauce

1. Using a small sharp knife, remove the fat and skin from the drumsticks. Discard the skin. Pat the fat dry with a paper towel and set aside.

2. Fill a medium saucepan with enough water to cover the chicken and bring to a boil over high heat. Add the drumsticks, ginger, and salt. Reduce the heat to medium and cook for about 25 minutes. Check for doneness by poking a chopstick into the thickest part of a drumstick. If the juice runs clear, then the meat is done. If it's still pink, cook for another 5 to 10 minutes. Transfer the drumsticks to a bowl of ice water. When cool enough to handle, bone and coarsely shred the chicken. Discard the bones and set the shredded meat aside.

3. In a small bowl, whisk the soy sauce, rice vinegar, and sugar until the sugar dissolves.

4. In a small saucepan, heat the reserved chicken fat over medium heat until it is rendered. (You can substitute vegetable oil.) Reduce the heat to low. Add the shallot and stir-fry until fragrant and slightly golden, about 1 minute. Add the soy sauce mixture and stir until combined, about 1 minute. Remove from the heat.

5. Distribute the phở noodles between two bowls. Add the chicken and herbs. Drizzle with the soy sauce mixture and stir to mix. Serve with hot chili sauce on the side.

Variation tip: *Crispy Fried Shallots* make a nice topping for this dish.

Cooking tip: The chicken stock made when cooking the chicken can be saved to use later in a soup or porridge.

Beef Pho Rolls *Phở Cuốn*

MAKES 10 ROLLS • PREP TIME: 15 MINUTES + 15 MINUTES TO MARINATE • COOK TIME: 5 MINUTES

Phở cuốn is a modern variation, but it's so loved that there's a whole village called Ngũ Xá in Hanoi whose people specialize in the dish. They use whole phở sheets (before cutting them into thin noodle strips) to wrap stir-fried beef and herbs. The rolls are usually served with sweet and sour fish sauce dip with slices of green papaya in the sauce bowl. As with any cuốn dish, each bite of phở cuốn is a refreshing combination of meat, herbs, noodles, and sweet and sour dipping sauce.

1 small carrot, peeled and thinly sliced

½ kohlrabi, peeled, halved, and thinly sliced, or 1 English cucumber, thinly sliced

1 teaspoon salt

1 tablespoon sugar

1 tablespoon rice vinegar or freshly squeezed lime juice

8 ounces beef tenderloin or flank steak, thinly sliced against the grain

2 tablespoons vegetable oil, divided

1 tablespoon fish sauce

1½ teaspoons freshly ground black pepper

1 tablespoon minced garlic

10 fresh rice noodle sheets

1 cup fresh cilantro leaves

1 cup fresh mint leaves

1 cup fresh Thai/Asian basil leaves or regular basil leaves

2 recipes Sweet and Sour Fish Sauce Dip

1. In a bowl, toss the carrot and kohlrabi with the salt. Let sit for 10 minutes. Rinse and squeeze out the excess water. Add the sugar and vinegar and mix well. Set the pickles aside to marinate for at least 15 minutes.

2. In another large bowl, toss the beef with 1 tablespoon of oil, the fish sauce and the pepper. Mix well.

3. Heat a sauté pan over high heat. Swirl in the remaining 1 tablespoon of oil to spread it evenly. Add the garlic and beef and stir-fry until the beef is almost brown, about 1 minute. Remove the pan from the heat.

4. Spread out a noodle sheet on a platter or cutting board. Starting from the edge closest to you, scatter on some fresh herbs. Add a few slices of beef and roll it up. Repeat with the remaining phở sheets, herbs, and meat.

5. Cut each roll into bite-size pieces, if desired.

6. Add ½ cup of the kohlrabi and carrot pickles (if using) to the dipping sauce and serve.

Variation tip: Phở sheets are similar to fresh noodle sheets in Asian stores. If you can't find them, substitute 7 ounces dry phở noodles and make it a salad bowl. The presentation will be different, but equally tasty.

Red Wine Beef Stew Pho *Phở Sốt Vang*

SERVES 2 • PREP TIME: 10 MINUTES • COOK TIME: 1 HOUR

*This phở version, which is available exclusively on Hanoi streets, is inspired by French beef stew in red wine (see **Baguette with Beef in Red Wine Stew**). I first ate phở sốt vang when I moved to Hanoi for college and fell in love with it instantly. Unlike the clean classic phở broth, phở sốt vang broth is sophisticated, with many layers of flavors. The elaborate beef broth and the complex flavor of warm spices partner well with flat rice noodles, making it a treat, especially in wintertime.*

1 pound boneless ribeye steak, cut into ⅓-inch pieces

1 tablespoon five-spice powder

2 tablespoons salt, divided

1 (750 ml) bottle red wine

4 tablespoons vegetable oil, divided

2 tablespoons minced garlic, divided

2 sweet onions, finely chopped

1 pound beefsteak tomatoes, finely chopped

1 tablespoon fish sauce

7 ounces dry phở noodles, cooked according to package instructions (or see here)

1 cup fresh Thai/Asian basil leaves or cilantro leaves, coarsely chopped

Freshly ground black pepper

Hot chili sauce

1. In a large bowl, toss the beef with the five-spice powder, 1 tablespoon of salt, and 2 tablespoons of red wine. Set aside to marinate while you prepare the vegetables.

2. Heat a large sauté pan over high heat for 2 minutes. Swirl in 2 tablespoons of oil to spread it evenly. Add 1 tablespoon of garlic and stir-fry until slightly golden and fragrant, about 30 seconds. Add the onions and stir-fry for 2 minutes. Add the tomatoes and the remaining 1 tablespoon of salt and stir-fry until the tomatoes and onions become a paste, about 3 minutes. Transfer the paste to a medium saucepan and set aside.

3. Swirl the remaining 2 tablespoons of oil in the sauté pan to spread it evenly. Add the remaining 1 tablespoon of garlic and the beef and stir-fry for 1 minute. Transfer the beef to the saucepan with the tomato-onion paste.

4. Pour the remaining red wine into the saucepan and stir well. Bring to a boil over medium-high heat. Reduce the heat to low and simmer for 1 hour. Turn off the heat and add the fish sauce. Stir well to mix.

5. Distribute the noodles between two bowls. Ladle the hot stock and meat over the noodles. Sprinkle with the chopped herbs and serve with pepper and hot chili sauce on the side.

Substitution tip: You can replace the five-spice powder in this recipe with 1 tablespoon ground cinnamon and 5 whole cloves.

Ingredient tip: The red wine doesn't have to be a fancy one. It should be on the sweeter side. (I usually use a Côtes du Lot Malbec, which is about $8.)

Butternut Squash and Salmon Porridge

Chapter Six

Cháo
PORRIDGE

Chicken Porridge   *Cháo Gà*

Butternut Squash and Salmon Porridge   *Cháo Bí Đỏ Cá Hồi*

Pork Rib Porridge   *Cháo Sườn*

Fish Porridge   *Cháo Cá*

Mushroom Porridge   *Cháo Nấm*

Clam Porridge   *Cháo Ngao*

Crispy Fried Shallots   *Hành Phi*

Chinese Fried Breadsticks / Doughnuts   *Quẩy/Giò Chéo Quẩy*

Cháo, **meaning porridge or congee,** is pronounced "chow" as in "chowder." Super easy, right? This rice-based stew is among Vietnam's oldest foods, so as you can imagine we have a lot of idioms, folk tales, and metaphors related to this food. Most Vietnamese children eat cháo before learning to eat more solid foods. However, cháo is not only for children. It's also a favorite for adults and considered a remedy for a cold, flu, or other sickness. The main ingredients are rice and stock or water. Then depending on the kind of cháo, we may add beans, meats, or seafood. Vietnamese people eat porridge with a lot of herbs—mainly scallions and herbs with warm medicinal properties like red shiso or perilla leaves.

My mother and grandparents remember resorting to cháo during difficult times when there was not enough to eat. They would add a lot of water to a handful of moldy rice, along with tasteless root vegetables like banana roots, old kohlrabi, or cassava to fill their stomachs temporarily. Luckily, I got to know cháo during peacetime, and it is considered a nutritious and satisfying food that is very light and easy to digest. Cháo is a common breakfast street food option, and some cháo vendors offer crispy Chinese breadsticks or doughnuts for diners to order on the side. Cháo is easy to cook at home, so it's helpful for busy cooks, especially on rainy days and in cold weather. Basically you just toss all the ingredients together in a pot and simmer until they're combined into a thick, smooth soup. Meat and other protein choices are usually stir fried to be more flavorful and to add a nice contrast to the mild, comforting rice soup. Traditionally we soak the rice for a few hours or overnight so it cooks faster. However, as a spontaneous cook who doesn't usually plan meals ahead of time, I don't often soak my rice.

When cooking porridge, it's okay to use a very small amount of salt. It's much easier to add more salt or fish sauce while serving than to try and fix an overly salted pot of cháo. Also, note that the water and rice ratio in this chapter is for medium thickness. If you want it to be more watery, simply add more boiling water toward the end. Finally, when eating cháo, a rule of thumb is to start by eating around the edge of the bowl because it's the coolest part. Cháo is famous for retaining heat for a long time, and the center of the bowl can be so hot that it might burn your tongue.

Chicken Porridge *Cháo Gà*

SERVES 4 • PREP TIME: 5 MINUTES • COOK TIME: 1 HOUR

*Chicken porridge in Vietnam is like chicken soup in the West. It's a warm comfort food for rainy days and for when you have a cold. Every family has their own way of cooking chicken porridge. In this recipe, I add diced potatoes and carrots, a tip that I learned from my best friend, Dương, who used to cook chicken porridge for me when I was sick. The potatoes and carrots add more texture and natural sweetness to the porridge. When we eat cháo gà on the street, quẩy, or **Chinese Fried Breadsticks/Doughnuts**, are usually available to order on the side.*

2 pounds chicken drumsticks, skin removed

1 (2-inch) piece ginger, lightly smashed

1 onion, halved

3 teaspoons salt, divided

4¼ cups water

¼ cup jasmine rice

¼ cup glutinous rice (also known as sticky rice or sweet rice)

½ cup diced potato

½ cup diced carrot

1 teaspoon fish sauce

5 scallions, chopped

1 cup fresh perilla leaves or cilantro leaves, chopped

Freshly ground black pepper

1. In a saucepan, combine the chicken, ginger, onion, and 1 teaspoon of salt. Add the water and bring to a boil over high heat. Skim off the foam with a fine-mesh skimmer.

2. Add the rice, potato, and carrot, stir well, and return to a boil. Reduce the heat to low and cook for 1 hour, stirring occasionally to prevent the rice from sticking to the bottom of the pan. Turn off the heat. Remove the chicken and set aside to cool. Cover the saucepan and let it sit on the stove.

3. When the chicken is cool enough to handle, shred the meat with a knife or your hands. Return the meat to the pot. Season the porridge with the fish sauce and the remaining 2 teaspoons of salt. Mix well.

4. To serve, ladle the porridge into large bowls. Add the chopped scallions and perilla leaves and season with pepper.

Ingredient tip: Instead of drumsticks, you can use any part of the chicken that you like. Also, to avoid discoloration, keep the diced potato submerged in cool water until ready to use.

Butternut Squash and Salmon Porridge
Cháo Bí Đỏ Cá Hồi

SERVES 4 • PREP TIME: 10 MINUTES • COOK TIME: 1 HOUR

Butternut squash and pumpkin are favorite vegetables in Vietnam. We love them so much that we don't let any part escape us — we eat the leaves, stems, blossoms, and fruits! When I lived in America, I cooked butternut squash soup when it was in season. However, since I moved back to Vietnam, I've stopped making it because soup with cream is a little heavy for the tropical heat here. That's why I decided to try my hand at butternut squash porridge. I chose salmon for the topping because the mild flavor and buttery texture of stir-fried salmon cubes really enhance the natural sweetness of butternut squash.

4¼ cups chicken stock or water

1½ cups butternut squash cubes

¼ cup jasmine rice

¼ cup glutinous rice (also known as sticky rice or sweet rice)

1 tablespoon salt, plus more if necessary

2 pounds salmon fillets, cut into ¾-inch cubes

3 tablespoons soy sauce

1 teaspoon freshly ground black pepper

3 tablespoons vegetable oil

5 scallions, chopped, white parts and green parts separated

Freshly ground black pepper

1 recipe [Crispy Fried Shallots](#) (optional)

1. Bring the chicken stock to a boil in a saucepan over medium-high heat.

2. Add the butternut squash and rice. Return to a boil, then reduce the heat to low. Cook for 45 minutes, stirring once every 15 minutes to make sure the rice doesn't stick to the bottom of the pan. Turn off the heat. Cover the pan and let it sit on the stove for 15 minutes. Stir in the salt.

3. Meanwhile, season the salmon with the soy sauce and pepper.

4. Heat a medium sauté pan over high heat. Swirl in the oil to spread it evenly. Add the white parts of the scallions and stir-fry for 30 seconds. Add the salmon and stir-fry for 1 minute. Stop stirring and let the salmon cook until nicely brown, about 1 minute more.

5. Ladle the porridge into bowls. Add the salmon. Scatter the chopped scallion greens on the salmon, season with pepper, and top with the shallots (if using). Serve immediately.

Ingredient tip: I usually reserve the simple chicken stock left over from boiling chicken for Chicken and Cabbage Salad to make this porridge.

Pork Rib Porridge *Cháo Sườn*

SERVES 4 • PREP TIME: 10 MINUTES • COOK TIME: 1 HOUR 10 MINUTES

When I was little, my mother would pick me up from school every afternoon and drive me to the local market on her bike to buy rib porridge for my younger brother. On the way home, I would pray for him to not finish his portion so I could "help" him. Rib porridge is popular street food in the North, where it is loved by adults and children alike. Adults without children usually eat the porridge right there on the street, and those with children order take-away. Like chicken porridge, many people like to eat this dish with Chinese doughnuts for a crunchy texture, but it's absolutely delicious just the way it is.

- 7 ounces rice flour
- 1½ tablespoons salt, divided
- 2 pounds pork ribs, cut into 1½ inch pieces
- 2 tablespoons fish sauce, plus more if necessary
- 1 teaspoon freshly ground black pepper, plus more if necessary
- 2 tablespoons vegetable oil
- 1 tablespoon minced shallot
- 1 recipe Chinese Fried Breadsticks/Doughnuts (optional)

1. In a large bowl, mix the rice flour with 2½ cups of water. Stir well. Set aside for 30 minutes to 1 hour while you cook the ribs.
2. Fill a large saucepan with water and add ½ tablespoon of salt. Bring to a boil over high heat. Add the ribs and return to a boil. Cook for 5 minutes, then turn off the heat. Drain the ribs and rinse under running water. Drain again. Rinse the saucepan.

3. Pour 4¼ cups of water into the same saucepan and add the remaining 1 tablespoon of salt and the ribs. Bring to a boil over high heat. Skim off the foam with a fine-mesh skimmer. Reduce the heat to low and cook for 1 hour. Transfer the ribs to a bowl. Season the ribs with the fish sauce and pepper.

4. Bring the rib stock back to a boil over high heat. Reduce the heat to medium. Stir up the rice flour batter and pour it into the boiling stock. Stir constantly until it becomes a gelatinous porridge, like yogurt. Turn off the heat, cover, and let it sit on the stove.

5. Heat a medium sauté pan over high heat. Swirl in the oil to spread it evenly. Add the shallot and stir-fry for 30 seconds. Add the ribs and stir-fry for 2 minutes. Remove from the heat.

6. Heat the porridge over medium heat. Transfer the ribs to the porridge saucepan. Stir constantly until the porridge bubbles. Turn off the heat. Add more fish sauce if necessary.

7. Serve immediately with freshly ground black pepper and breadsticks or doughnuts, if desired.

Substitution tip: *You can substitute jasmine rice for the rice flour. Soak the rice in water for an hour, then drain the rice and transfer to a blender. Blend finely with 2½ cups water and set aside as in step 1.*

Fish Porridge *Cháo Cá*

SERVES 4 • PREP TIME: 15 MINUTES + 1 HOUR TO SOAK • COOK TIME: 45 MINUTES

On winter evenings when we finished work late, my best friend and co-worker Dương and I would hop on our scooters to a fish porridge vendor quite a distance away. Despite the howling wind, the place was always packed, and the air warm and cozy with the aroma of ginger, pepper, and fried shallots. We'd wrap our hands around the hot bowls to warm them up. The rich fish bone stock, freshly caught fish that melted like butter, and soft-leaf greens that absorbed all the flavors made each bite a treasure. The best vegetable for fish porridge is garland chrysanthemum, available in most Chinatowns or Asian markets.

- ½ cup jasmine rice
- ¼ cup glutinous rice (also known as sticky rice or sweet rice)
- 4¼ cups water
- 1 onion, halved
- 4 (2-inch) pieces ginger, 2 lightly smashed and 2 peeled and minced
- 2 teaspoons salt
- 3 pounds kingfish chunks with bones, ½ to 1 inch thick (or substitute mackerel or any firm white-flesh fish)
- 2 tablespoons fish sauce
- 1 teaspoon freshly ground black pepper, plus more if necessary
- 2 tablespoons vegetable oil
- 1 tablespoon minced shallot
- 2 cups fresh dill, chopped
- 1 cup chopped scallion
- 1 recipe Crispy Fried Shallots (optional)

1. Soak the rice in water for 1 hour. Drain well. Pound the rice using a mortar and pestle or coarsely chop it in a food processor.
2. Pour 4¼ cups of fresh water into a large saucepan and add the onion, smashed ginger, and salt. Bring to a boil over high heat. Add the fish and return the water to a boil. Transfer the fish to a bowl and let it cool. Add the rice to the fish stock and bring to a boil. Reduce the heat to low and cook for 30 minutes. Turn off the heat, cover, and let the pot sit on the stove for 15 minutes.
3. Bone the fish and discard the bones. Season the fish with the fish sauce, minced ginger, and pepper.
4. Heat a sauté pan over high heat. Swirl in the oil to spread it evenly. Add the minced shallot and the fish and stir-fry for 1 minute. Remove the pan from the heat.
5. Bring the porridge to a boil over medium heat, stirring occasionally. Add the fish to the porridge and lightly stir to combine.
6. To serve, distribute the dill among four bowls. Ladle the porridge over the dill. Sprinkle with the scallions and shallots (if using). Serve with additional black pepper.

Ingredient tip: Instead of bone-in fish pieces, you can use fish fillets—just skip the boiling step.

Mushroom Porridge
Cháo Nấm

SERVES 3 • PREP TIME: 10 MINUTES • COOK TIME: 1 HOUR

The first time I tried this dish was a rainy summer night in Saigon years ago. My friend took me to her favorite vegan restaurant in the city and insisted that this dish was a must-try. She was right — it was hard for me to resist a second bowl! The porridge was light but hearty, and the assorted mushrooms created a satisfying combination of crunchy and meaty textures. Mushroom porridge is common in many vegan restaurants in the South.

¼ cup jasmine rice

¼ cup glutinous rice (also known as sticky rice or sweet rice)

¼ cup mung beans (also known as yellow beans, optional)

3½ cups water

2 teaspoons salt

7 ounces enoki mushrooms, trimmed of roots

5 ounces clamshell mushrooms (also known as beech or shimeji mushrooms), trimmed of roots

1 pound shiitake mushrooms, stems removed

2 tablespoons light sesame oil

1 tablespoon minced ginger

1 tablespoon minced shallot

2 tablespoons soy sauce

1 cup fresh cilantro leaves, chopped

1 recipe Crispy Fried Shallots (optional)

Freshly ground black pepper

1. In a saucepan, combine the rice, beans (if using), water, and salt. Bring to a boil over high heat, stirring to prevent the rice from sticking to the bottom. Reduce the heat to low and simmer for 1 hour, stirring occasionally.
2. Meanwhile, soak the mushrooms in lightly salted water for 10 minutes, then gently rinse with fresh water. Drain well. Shred the shiitake mushrooms into ½-inch strips.
3. Heat a medium sauté pan over high heat. Swirl in the oil to spread it evenly.
4. Add the ginger and shallot and stir-fry until slightly brown, about 1 minute. Add the mushrooms and soy sauce and stir-fry for 1 minute. Transfer the mushroom mixture to the porridge pot and stir gently to combine.
5. To serve, ladle the porridge into bowls. Sprinkle with the chopped cilantro and top with shallots (if using). Serve with black pepper.

Substitution tip: *You can use any mushroom you like—one kind or a mixture.*

Clam Porridge *Cháo Ngao*

SERVES 3 OR 4 • PREP TIME: 10 MINUTES • COOK TIME: 1 HOUR

Clam porridge is on the menus of many small restaurants along beaches in the north of Vietnam. We like to top this with a lot of rau răm *(Vietnamese coriander/Vietnamese mint) to add warmth (yang) and to balance the cold element (yin) in clams.* Rau răm *is a staple herb in Vietnamese stores in Chinatowns, but you can substitute scallions and/or cilantro. If you like clam chowder, you'll love this porridge!*

3 pounds white clams

1 chile, lightly smashed

¼ cup glutinous rice (also known as sticky rice or sweet rice)

¼ cup jasmine rice

1 (2-inch) piece ginger, lightly smashed

½ teaspoon salt, plus more if necessary

2 teaspoons fish sauce

1 teaspoon freshly ground black pepper, plus more if necessary

2 tablespoons vegetable oil

2 tablespoons minced shallot

1 cup chopped scallion

1 cup fresh Vietnamese coriander leaves (optional)

1 recipe [Crispy Fried Shallots](#) (optional)

1. Soak the clams and hot chile in a large bowl of water for 20 minutes. Rinse the clams and drain well. Discard any clams that are open.

2. Pour 2½ cups of fresh water into a large saucepan. Add the clams and bring to a boil over high heat. The clams should all open; discard any that do not. Turn off the heat. Transfer the clams to a large bowl and let them cool enough to

handle. Strain the stock into another large bowl and discard any dirt or sand. Rinse out the saucepan and pour the strained stock back in.

3. Return the stock to a boil over high heat. Add the rice, ginger, and salt. Stir and bring back to a boil. Reduce the heat to low and simmer for 50 minutes, stirring occasionally. Turn off the heat, cover, and let the pot sit on the stove for 15 minutes.

4. Remove the clams from their shells. Toss the clams with the fish sauce and pepper.

5. Heat a medium sauté pan over high heat. Swirl in the oil to spread it evenly. Add the shallot and stir-fry until slightly golden, about 1 minute. Add the clams and stir-fry for 1 minute. Turn off the heat.

6. Stir the porridge and bring to a boil over medium heat. Ladle the porridge into bowls. Add the fried clams, chopped herbs, and shallots (if using). Stir to mix. Season with salt and pepper.

Substitution tip: *You can substitute mussels for the clams in this recipe.*

Crispy Fried Shallots
Hành Phi

MAKES ABOUT 2½ CUPS • PREP TIME: 10 MINUTES • COOK TIME: 10 MINUTES

Crispy fried shallots are an addictive and versatile topping that adds texture, flavor, and aroma to salads, steamed crêpes, sticky rice dishes, and, of course, porridge. You can make a big batch and store them in an airtight jar at room temperature for up to 3 months — if you can resist them that long. The aromatic oil left over from frying shallots can be used to toss with salad or to cook with.

8 ounces shallots, thinly sliced

Vegetable oil, for frying

1. Line a platter or baking sheet with a paper towel.
2. In a small saucepan, pour in oil to a depth of 1 inch. Heat the oil over medium heat until it reaches 390°F. (Check by dipping a chopstick into the oil. If it sizzles and bubbles, then it's ready.) Add about ½ cup of the shallots. The oil should cover the scallions. Reduce the heat to medium-low. Lightly stir in circular motions until the shallots are pale yellow. With a fine-mesh strainer or slotted spoon, transfer the shallots to the paper towel. Repeat with the remaining shallots.
3. Use immediately, or let the shallots cool completely before storing.

Variation tip: *To make a small batch, thinly slice 2 shallots. Mix the shallot slices with 1 teaspoon cornstarch or tapioca starch. Heat 3 tablespoons vegetable oil in a small saucepan. Add the shallots and fry over medium-low heat until lightly golden. Remove from the heat and drain on a paper towel.*

Cooking tip: *The shallot slices don't have to be too thin, but they should all be the same thickness in order to cook evenly. Fry the shallots in batches;*

crowding the shallots together in one batch can lower the oil temperature and make the shallots soggy.

Chinese Fried Breadsticks / Doughnuts *Quẩy/ ò Chéo Quẩy*

MAKES ABOUT 25 (4-INCH) STICKS • PREP TIME: 5 MINUTES + 5 HOURS RISING TIME COOK TIME: 25 MINUTES

This goodie, known as quẩy, is a Chinese influence in Vietnam and is featured at chicken and rib porridge vendors. Some phở vendors in Hanoi also offer quẩy on the side, a remnant of the war and postwar rationing period when Vietnam received wheat as food aid. Those who could afford phở also dipped Chinese doughnuts or cold baguettes into their bowl of meatless phở to make it more filling. Although eating phở with quẩy now might cause phở snobs to raise their eyebrows, quẩy pairs well with cháo because its crispiness complements the thick rice stew.

2 teaspoons baking soda

1 cup water, at room temperature, divided

1 teaspoon baking powder

3 1/3 cups all-purpose flour

2 teaspoons sugar

½ teaspoon salt

Vegetable oil, for frying

1. In a small bowl, whisk the baking soda into ¼ cup of water. In another small bowl, whisk the baking powder into ¼ cup of water.

2. In a mixing bowl, whisk together the flour, sugar, and salt. Add the baking soda water and baking powder water to the mixing bowl. Slowly pour in the

remaining ½ cup of water, stirring well with chopsticks or a spatula until combined. Add 1 to 2 tablespoons of water if the dough is too dry. Knead with your hands for about 3 minutes to form a rough dough. Cover and let the dough rest for 20 minutes.

3. Uncover and knead the dough again for about 2 minutes. Cover and let rest for 20 minutes.

4. Uncover and knead the dough a third time for about 2 minutes. The dough should be smooth. Cover and let rest for 20 minutes.

5. Uncover and flatten the dough to ½-inch thickness. Cover with a damp cloth and let it rise for 3 to 4 hours.

6. Uncover and flatten the dough into a rectangular shape, about ¼ inch thick and 2½ inches wide. Cut the dough crosswise into ¾-inch strips.

7. Dip a skewer or chopstick in water to prevent sticking. Press the skewer on the middle of one strip lengthwise, then place another strip on top. Press the skewer on the middle of the top strip lengthwise. Set aside. Repeat with the remaining strips.

8. In a medium saucepan or deep sauté pan, pour in the oil to a depth of about 2 inches. Heat the oil over medium heat until it reaches 390°F or above. (Test by dipping a chopstick into the oil. If the oil sizzles, then it's ready.)

9. Hold one dough stick (two strips pressed together) with both hands. Lightly pull two ends to stretch the length by half. After pulling, each stick should be about 3½ inches long. Gently drop it into the hot oil. Flip and submerge it in the oil. Keep flipping and submerging until the stick is fluffy and golden. If the center of the stick is too tight to fluff evenly, lightly part the two sides with chopsticks to loosen the middle. Remove from the oil and transfer to paper towels to drain.

Storage tip: These breadsticks can be frozen for 3 months. Defrost them in a microwave and crisp them in an oven or toaster before serving.

Stir-Fried Beef Bún Salad

Chapter Seven

Bún
RICE VERMICELLI

Rib Bún Soup *Bún Sườn*

Fish Bún Soup in Tomato and Dill Broth *Bún Cá*

Shrimp Bún Soup *Bún Tôm*

Vegetable Bún Soup *Bún Chay*

Beef Bún Soup *Bún Bò*

Stir-Fried Beef Bún Salad *Bún Bò Xào*

Vegan Stir-Fried Bún with Vegetables *Bún Xào Chay*

Grilled Pork Bún with Herbs and Sweet and Sour Dipping Sauce *Bún Chả*

Crispy Roasted Pork Bún Salad *Bún Thịt Quay*

Pan-Seared Duck Breast Bún Salad *Bún Vịt áp Chảo*

There are many kinds of rice noodles in Vietnam, with countless local varieties. However, all regions share their mutual love for bún, a thin, round rice noodle that has been around for more than a thousand years. Next to steamed rice, bún is the most commonly consumed rice-based food. The making of the bún noodle is a labor-intensive process that takes days. Rice is soaked in water for two days before being ground. The rice starch is then wrapped in cloth and hung to drain the water. Next, the starch is whipped into a thick paste and pressed through a machine into long strips. The noodles are quickly boiled before being delivered to noodle vendors in local markets. Freshly boiled bún is available in virtually all markets in Vietnam. The only choice overseas is dry packaged bún, but the good news is that it tastes authentic and takes only a few minutes to cook.

There are myriad ways to eat bún. Bún can be served with stock in a noodle soup or with sauce in a salad bowl. We also dip bún in dipping sauce or wrap bún in lettuce leaves or rice paper to make rolls. As with most Vietnamese dishes, it's common practice to serve bún with an abundance of fresh herbs. Unlike phở noodles, which we pair with beef or chicken only, the protein choices that go with bún are endless, from exotic snails and soft-shell crabs to tofu and mushrooms; anything you can think of will work. Because of its versatility, bún dishes are popular both at street food vendors and in home kitchens. Be it a big city or a rural marketplace in Vietnam, you'll stumble upon bún vendors every few minutes. For family meals, bún dishes can serve as an extravagant treat for weekend gatherings or a quick simple soup for dinners on busy weekdays.

Rib BÚN Soup *Bún Sườn*

SERVES 3 OR 4 • PREP TIME: 10 MINUTES • COOK TIME: 1 HOUR

This soup is popular for breakfast and lunch in the north of Vietnam. It's perfect in both the steaming summer heat and the bone-cutting winter chill. The stock is rich from simmered bones and mashed tomatoes, the ribs tender and well marinated, and the crunchy taro roots and fragrant herbs serve as the "cherry on top."

2 tablespoons salt, divided

3 pounds ribs, cut into 1½-inch pieces

1 onion, halved

1½ pounds taro root, peeled and thinly sliced diagonally

4¼ cups water

3 tablespoons fish sauce, divided

1 teaspoon ground turmeric

1½ teaspoons freshly ground black pepper

3 tablespoons vegetable oil, divided

3 tablespoons minced shallot

6 scallions, cut into 1-inch pieces, white parts and green parts separated

1½ pounds tomatoes, peeled and cut into thin wedges

10 ounces rice vermicelli, cooked according to package instructions (or see here)

6 saw-tooth herb leaves (also known as culantro), chopped, or 1 cup fresh Thai/Asian basil or cilantro leaves

Hot chili sauce

1. Fill a large saucepan with water and add 1 tablespoon of salt. Bring to a boil over high heat. Add the ribs and return to a boil. Drain the ribs and rinse under running water. Drain them again. Rinse out the saucepan.

2. Pour the 4¼ cups of fresh water into the saucepan and add the ribs and onion. Bring to a boil over high heat. Skim off any foam with a fine-mesh skimmer. Reduce the heat to low and simmer for 1 hour.

3. In a colander, sprinkle ½ tablespoon of salt over the taro. Wearing gloves, mix well and gently squeeze for about 3 minutes. Rinse the taro under running water, then squeeze out the excess water. Set aside.

4. Transfer the ribs to a large bowl; reserve the bone stock. Season the ribs with 1 tablespoon of fish sauce, the turmeric, and the pepper.

5. Heat a sauté pan over high heat. Swirl in 2 tablespoons of oil to spread it evenly. Add the shallot and stir-fry until fragrant, about 30 seconds. Reduce the heat to medium and add the ribs. Stir-fry for 3 minutes, then transfer the ribs to a bowl.

6. Heat the same sauté pan over high heat. Add the remaining 1 tablespoon of oil. Add the white parts of the scallion and stir-fry until slightly golden, about 1 minute. Add the tomatoes and the remaining ½ tablespoon of salt and stir-fry for 5 minutes. Turn off the heat.

7. Add the tomatoes to the bone stock and bring to a boil over medium-high heat. Add the taro. Bring to a boil again, then turn off the heat. Season with the remaining 2 tablespoons of fish sauce.

8. To serve, distribute the rice vermicelli into bowls. Add the ribs, chopped herbs, and scallion greens. Ladle enough stock mixture into each bowl to cover the vermicelli. Serve immediately with hot sauce on the side.

Substitution tip: *If you can't find taro, omit it or substitute any greens that you fancy. The stock and the ribs are the soul of this dish.*

Fish BÚN Soup in Tomato and Dill Broth *Bún Cá*

SERVES 2 • PREP TIME: 10 MINUTES • COOK TIME: 15 MINUTES

This northern version of fish soup contains the distinctive turmeric and dill condiments. I learned it from a vendor who was selling it in my neighborhood in Hanoi. When I moved overseas, this soup was something I cooked for dinner on busy days.

1 pound white fish fillets, cut into bite-size pieces

1½ tablespoons salt, divided

1 teaspoon freshly ground black pepper

1 teaspoon ground turmeric

5 tablespoons vegetable oil, divided

2 tablespoons minced shallot

2 pounds tomatoes, cut into thin wedges

4¼ cups water

5 scallions, chopped

1 bunch fresh dill, coarsely chopped

1 tablespoon fish sauce, plus more for serving

7 ounces rice vermicelli, cooked according to package instructions (or see here)

Hot chili sauce, for serving

1. In a bowl, season the fish with ½ tablespoon of salt, the pepper, and turmeric. Gently stir to mix. Set aside.

2. Heat a large saucepan over high heat. Swirl in 2 tablespoons of oil to spread it evenly. Add the shallot and stir-fry until lightly golden, about 30 seconds. Add the tomatoes and the remaining 1 tablespoon of salt. Stir-fry until the tomatoes are smashed, about 4 minutes. Add the water, stir well, and bring to a boil. Add the scallions and dill. Turn off the heat and stir in the fish sauce.

3. Heat a medium sauté pan over high heat. Swirl in the remaining 3 tablespoons of oil to spread it evenly. Add the fish and fry until nicely brown, 2 to 3 minutes per side.

4. To serve, distribute the rice vermicelli into bowls. Add the fish, then ladle in the hot broth. Serve with fish sauce and hot chili sauce on the side.

> **Cooking tip:** *The stock will be even more flavorful if you can buy fish bones and heads to add to it.*

Shrimp Bún Soup *Bún Tôm*

SERVES 2 • PREP TIME: 15 MINUTES • COOK TIME: 20 MINUTES

This noodle soup originates from Hải Phòng, a big northern port city known for its seafood. It's also my best friend's hometown, so I used to visit several times a year. It was something that I looked forward to eating, both on the street and in her mother's kitchen.

4¼ cups water

1 pound large shrimp, peeled and deveined, shells and heads reserved

1 onion, halved

1 (2-inch) piece ginger, lightly smashed

2 beefsteak tomatoes, cut into wedges

3 tablespoons fish sauce, divided, plus more if necessary

1 bunch watercress, cut into 2- to 3-inch pieces

3 ounces pork tenderloin, thinly sliced (optional)

1 teaspoon freshly ground black pepper, plus more if necessary

6 dried or fresh shiitake or other mushrooms (optional)

1 ounce dried wood ear mushrooms (optional)

2 tablespoons vegetable oil

1 tablespoon minced shallot

7 ounces rice vermicelli, cooked according to package instructions (or see here)

1 cup fresh cilantro leaves or dill, coarsely chopped

2 scallions, chopped

Salt

1. In a medium saucepan, bring the water to a boil over high heat. Add the chopped shrimp shells and heads, onion, and ginger. Return to a boil. Skim off

any foam with a fine-mesh skimmer. Reduce the heat to low and simmer for 15 minutes.

2. Strain the stock through a fine-mesh strainer into a large bowl. Pour the strained stock back into the saucepan. Add the tomato wedges. Bring to a boil over high heat. Season with 1½ tablespoons of fish sauce. Add the watercress. Submerge the vegetables in the stock. Cook for 1 minute, then turn off the heat.

3. In a large bowl, toss together the shrimp, pork (if using), the remaining 1½ tablespoons of fish sauce, and the black pepper. Set aside to marinate.

4. If using dried mushrooms, soak them in boiling water for 10 minutes. Drain and rinse under running water. Trim off the hard ends. Squeeze out the excess water and thinly slice.

5. Heat the oil in a sauté pan over high heat. Add the shallot and stir-fry for 30 seconds. Add the shrimp, pork, and mushrooms. Stir-fry until the shrimp and pork are golden brown, 3 to 5 minutes.

6. To serve, distribute the rice vermicelli into bowls. Add the pork, shrimp, mushrooms, chopped herbs, scallions, and vegetables from the stockpot. Ladle the hot stock over to cover the rice vermicelli. Serve immediately with salt and pepper on the side.

Substitution tip: *Instead of watercress, you can use bok choy, yu choy, or any seasonal leafy greens.*

Vegetable Bún Soup *Bún Ch*

SERVES 4 • PREP TIME: 10 MINUTES • COOK TIME: 45 MINUTES

My late grandmother, like most Vietnamese, was Buddhist. After she retired, she went to pagodas every day to help with chores, including cooking vegan meals for charity and for the monthly full moon celebration. This hearty vegan soup is one of the many recipes she passed on to me. It can be eaten anytime, but it's especially satisfying after big parties and holidays, when much meat is consumed.

4¼ cups water

2 onions, halved

2 medium carrots, cut crosswise into 1-inch chunks

1 large daikon, cut crosswise into 1-inch chunks

½ pineapple, cut into 1-inch cubes

1 (2-inch) piece ginger, lightly smashed

1½ tablespoons salt, plus more if necessary

1 (10-ounce) block firm tofu

¼ cup vegetable oil

1 pound enoki or oyster mushrooms, roots trimmed

10 ounces rice vermicelli, cooked according to package instructions (or see here)

1 cup fresh cilantro leaves, chopped

Soy sauce, for serving

Hot chili sauce, for serving

1. Pour the water into a large saucepan. Add the onions, carrots, daikon, pineapple, ginger, and salt. Bring to a boil over high heat. Reduce the heat to low and simmer for 45 minutes.

2. Meanwhile, pat the tofu dry with a paper towel, the drier, the better to reduce spattering when frying. Cut the tofu into ½-inch pieces.

3. Heat a medium sauté pan over medium-high heat. Swirl in the oil to spread it evenly. Add the tofu and fry until golden on the bottom, about 7 minutes. Flip and fry the other side until golden, about 5 minutes.

4. Add the fried tofu and mushrooms to the stock. Bring to a boil over high heat, then turn off the heat.

5. Distribute the noodles into bowls. Pour the hot stock with tofu and mushroom over the noodles. Sprinkle with the cilantro. Serve hot with soy sauce and chili sauce on the side.

Variation tip: *Without the vermicelli, this recipe makes a good vegetable soup.*

Beef Bún Soup *Bún Bò*

SERVES 6 • PREP TIME: 20 MINUTES • COOK TIME: 1 HOUR 15 MINUTES

This spicy noodle soup is known in America as bún bò Huế in honor of Huế, a city in the central region. However, in Huế and other nearby cities, it's simply called bún bò, meaning beef bún. The stock has a complex flavor from the simmered bones, meat, and lemongrass. Bún bò is often served with homemade lemongrass chili oil, which adds another layer of depth and spiciness. It is so popular that the city of Huế recently asked to patent it — a request other cities strongly opposed because they wanted to keep the soup, too.

FOR THE CHILI OIL (OPTIONAL)

3 tablespoons vegetable oil

3 tablespoons minced lemongrass

2 tablespoons minced shallot

1 tablespoon red pepper flakes or fresh minced hot chile

Pinch salt

FOR THE SOUP

1½ tablespoons salt, divided

2 pounds pork bones

2 beef shanks (about 1 pound each)

1 pound sliced pork hocks (optional)

5 lemongrass stalks, smashed and bunched together

1 onion, halved

2 tablespoons shrimp paste

¼ cup water

2 tablespoons fish sauce, plus more if necessary

1½ pounds rice vermicelli, cooked according to package instructions (or see here)

½ onion, thinly sliced (optional)

1 cup fresh Thai/Asian basil leaves or cilantro

To make the chili oil (if using)

1. Heat a small saucepan over high heat. Swirl in the oil and reduce the heat to low.

2. Add the lemongrass and shallot and stir-fry for 2 minutes. Add the red pepper flakes and salt and stir-fry until the mixture becomes smooth and well combined, 2 to 3 minutes. Remove the pan from the heat and set aside.

To make the soup

1. Fill a large stockpot with water and add 1 tablespoon of salt. Add the pork bones, beef shanks, and pork hocks (if using). Bring to a boil over high heat. Turn off the heat. Drain the bones and meat under running water. Drain again. Rinse the pot.

2. Return the bones and meat to the pot. Add the lemongrass, onion, and remaining ½ tablespoon of salt. Add enough water to cover. Bring to a boil over high heat, skimming off any foam with a fine-mesh skimmer. Reduce the heat to low and simmer for 1 hour.

3. Remove the beef shanks and let them cool. Thinly slice them and set aside.

4. In a bowl, mix the fine shrimp paste into ¼ cup fresh water, stirring well to combine. Set aside for 10 minutes. The dregs will sink to the bottom.

5. After simmering for an hour, return the stock to a boil over high heat. Ladle the clear water from the fine shrimp paste bowl into the pot, discarding the dregs. Season the stock with the fish sauce.

6. To serve, distribute the rice vermicelli into big bowls. Add the beef and pork hocks. Add the onion slices (if using). Ladle in the hot stock. Add the basil. Drizzle with hot chili oil.

Substitution tip: *If you can't find fine shrimp paste or if you find the smell a little too strong, omit it. The dish won't have the distinctive aroma of the central region, but it will still be a delicious bún bò. Substitute store-bought hot chili sauce for homemade chili oil if you don't have time to make it.*

Stir-Fried Beef Bún Salad *Bún Bò Xào*

SERVES 2 OR 3 • PREP TIME: 20 MINUTES • COOK TIME: 5 MINUTES

This southern-style salad is very popular in Hanoi. Fresh vegetables and savory beef combine to create a delicious salad with complex flavors that are suitable all year round. It's delicious eaten on the street, but to me this salad is a dish that's better homemade, because I can control the tenderness of the beef and add extra fresh herbs or crispy fried shallots so it turns out just the way I like.

8 ounces beef tenderloin, thinly sliced against the grain

3 tablespoons vegetable oil, divided

1½ tablespoons soy sauce

1½ teaspoons freshly ground black pepper

2 tablespoons minced garlic

7 ounces rice vermicelli, cooked according to package instructions (or see here)

1 small cucumber, shredded

1 small carrot, shredded

1 cup fresh Thai/Asian basil leaves

1 cup fresh cilantro leaves

1 cup fresh mint leaves

1 cup roasted peanuts, coarsely chopped

2 recipes Sweet and Sour Fish Sauce Dip

½ cup Crispy Fried Shallots (optional)

1. Season the beef with 1 tablespoon of oil, the soy sauce, and pepper.
2. Heat a sauté pan over high heat. Swirl in the remaining 2 tablespoons of oil to spread it evenly. Add the garlic and stir-fry for 30 seconds. Add the beef and stir-

fry until brown, 1 to 2 minutes.

3. To assemble, in a large bowl, combine the vermicelli, cucumber, carrot, herbs, most of the peanuts (reserve some for garnish), and the beef.

4. Before serving, drizzle with the fish sauce dip and mix well. Top with the shallots (if using) and the remaining peanuts.

> **Ingredient tip:** This dish is also delicious with Carrot and Daikon Pickles, but if you add this, omit the cucumber and carrot.

Vegan Stir-Fried BÚn With Vegetables *Bún Xào Ch*

SERVES 2 • PREP TIME: 15 MINUTES + 30 MINUTES TO SOAK • COOK TIME: 15 MINUTES

When I moved to New York for school, my roommates/landladies were two lovely Chinese-Vietnamese Americans. They cooked every day, including elaborate vegan meals twice a month. I learned a lot about southern Vietnamese cooking from them. This vegan stir-fried rice vermicelli was something they would cook for potluck parties. They told me their American friends loved it. Following their lead, I also cooked this dish for potluck parties, and it was always a big hit.

5 tablespoons vegetable oil, divided

8 ounces string beans, thinly sliced diagonally

1 carrot, peeled and shredded

2 tablespoons minced garlic, divided

1½ teaspoons salt

10 ounces dry rice vermicelli, cooked according to package instructions (or see here)

2 tablespoons soy sauce

1½ teaspoons freshly ground black pepper

½ cup fresh cilantro leaves, coarsely chopped

½ cup roasted peanuts, chopped

1. Heat a large sauté pan over high heat. Swirl in 3 tablespoons of oil to spread it evenly. Add the beans, carrot, 1 tablespoon of garlic, and salt. Stir-fry until the

vegetables reach the desired softness. Transfer to a bowl.

2. In the same sauté pan, heat the remaining 2 tablespoons of oil. Add the remaining 1 tablespoon of garlic and the rice vermicelli. Stir-fry for 1 minute. Stir in the soy sauce and stir-fry until the noodles reach the desired softness, 3 to 5 minutes. If the noodles appear too dry, add 1 or 2 tablespoons of water while stir-frying. Add the vegetables and stir-fry for 2 minutes. Turn off the heat.

3. Sprinkle with the pepper, cilantro, and peanuts. Mix well and serve.

***Storage tip:** This dish can be kept in the refrigerator for up to 3 days. Reheat in a microwave for 1 minute or stir-fry over high heat for about 5 minutes.*

Grilled Pork Bún With Herbs and Sweet and Sour Dipping Sauce *Bún Chả*

SERVES 6 • PREP TIME: 30 MINUTES + 1 HOUR TO MARINATE • COOK TIME: 30 MINUTES

Bún chả is a popular northern street food and a common lunch choice in Hanoi. Many people like to cook bún chả on weekends for family gatherings, especially during the summer. During his 2015 visit to Vietnam, President Barack Obama dined at a bún chả vendor. After that, a lot of bún chả places named "Obama" popped up throughout the country. This is one of my favorite bún variations, and it's always the first thing I eat when I'm back in Hanoi. Many vendors offer two options of meat: slices, which is the classic, and patties, a later addition.

FOR THE SAUCE

2½ cups water

¾ cup freshly squeezed lime juice or rice vinegar

½ cup fish sauce

¾ cup sugar

2 tablespoons minced garlic

2 tablespoons minced hot chile

FOR THE PICKLES (OPTIONAL)

1 small carrot, peeled and thinly sliced

½ kohlrabi, peeled and thinly sliced, or 1 English cucumber, thinly sliced

1 teaspoon salt

1 tablespoon sugar

1 tablespoon rice vinegar or freshly squeezed lime juice

FOR THE PORK SLICES (CHA MIENG)

1 pound pork shoulder, thinly sliced against the grain

2 tablespoons minced shallot

2 tablespoons minced garlic

2 tablespoons fish sauce

1½ tablespoons honey

1½ teaspoons freshly ground black pepper

Vegetable oil, if pan-grilling

FOR THE PORK PATTIES (CHA VIÊN)

1 pound pork shoulder, finely chopped

2 tablespoons minced shallot

2 tablespoons minced garlic

2 tablespoons fish sauce

1½ tablespoons honey

1½ teaspoons freshly ground black pepper

Vegetable oil, if pan-grilling

FOR SERVING

1½ pounds rice vermicelli, cooked according to package instructions (or see here)

1 cup fresh cilantro leaves

1 cup fresh mint leaves

1 cup fresh Thai/Asian basil leaves (optional)

1 cup fresh perilla leaves (optional)

To make the sauce

In a large bowl, whisk the water, lime juice, fish sauce, and sugar until the sugar dissolves. Stir in the garlic and hot chiles. Set aside.

To make the pickles (if using)

1. In a bowl, toss together the carrot, kohlrabi, and salt. Let sit for 10 minutes.
2. Rinse and squeeze out the excess water. Add the sugar and vinegar. Mix well.
3. Set aside to marinate for at least 15 minutes.

To make the chả

1. For the pork slices, in a large bowl, toss together the sliced pork, shallot, garlic, fish sauce, honey, and pepper.
2. For the patties, repeat step 1 with the ground pork in a separate bowl.
3. Cover both bowls and let the pork marinate in the refrigerator for at least 1 hour or overnight.
4. For patties, shape the ground meat into 1-inch meatballs and lightly flatten them to ½-inch-thick patties.
5. Grill the pork slices and patties separately. There are three ways to grill chả:

Charcoal grill (traditional Vietnamese way) Char-grill the meat slices for about 5 minutes on each side until nicely golden brown. Char-grill the patties for 7 to 10 minutes on each side.

Pan grill

For slices: Heat a sauté pan over high heat for about 2 minutes. Brush the pan with a thin layer of oil. Add the pork slices and cook on one side until nicely golden brown, 1 to 2 minutes. Flip and cook the other side until nicely golden, 1 to 2 minutes. Remove from the heat.

For patties: Heat the sauté pan over high heat. Brush with a thin layer of oil, then reduce the heat to medium. Add the meat patties and cook for 3 minutes on one side. Increase the heat to high and cook until golden brown, 1 to 2 minutes. Reduce the heat to medium, flip, and repeat on the other side.

Roast Preheat the oven to 425°F. Roast the slices for 10 to 15 minutes and the patties for about 20 minutes.

To serve

Distribute the rice vermicelli and herbs on plates. In a big bowl, ladle the sauce to half full. Add the pork slices and pork patties. Add the pickles (if using). Dip a bit of vermicelli and herbs into the sauce bowl and eat with the grilled pork all in one bite.

> ***Serving tip:*** *You can also arrange the vermicelli, meat, herbs, and pickles in a big bowl and pour nước chấm over it like in a salad. This way is simpler, and there are fewer dishes to wash.*

Crispy Roasted Pork BÚn Salad *Bún Thit Qu*

SERVES 2 • PREP TIME: 10 MINUTES • COOK TIME: 1 HOUR

This refreshing, savory salad bowl combines soft rice noodles, crispy pork, and crunchy herbs with sweet and sour lime, garlic, and chili fish sauce dressing. When I was small, my mom used to buy crispy roasted pork on the last day of the month when she got her salary. These pork chunks were always hung up at the vendors' stalls, and I could smell the mouthwatering aroma of roasted meat and five-spice powder from far away. My mom would ask the vendor to give me the two crispiest and brownest pieces to test. I would always start with the tender, juicy meat and save the golden crackling (the best part) for last.

1 pound pork belly

1½ teaspoons salt, divided, plus more to cover the pork

1½ teaspoons five-spice powder

1 tablespoon soy sauce

1½ teaspoons rice vinegar

7 ounces rice vermicelli, cooked according to package instructions (or see here)

2 cups fresh basil, cilantro, mint, or perilla leaves

2 recipes Sweet and Sour Fish Sauce Dip

1. Preheat the oven to 425°F. Bring a kettle of water to a boil.

2. Place the pork, skin-side down, in a large saucepan. Add ½ teaspoon of salt. Pour enough boiling water over the meat to cover it, and bring to a boil over high heat. Turn off the heat. Drain and rinse the pork under running water. Drain again and pat dry with a paper towel.

3. Using a fork, puncture the pork skin a few times. Don't puncture too deep into the fat layer, or the fat will splash when roasting. Flip the meat and make crosswise cuts about ½ inch deep into the meat, leaving 1-inch gaps between cuts.

4. In a small bowl, mix the five-spice powder and soy sauce. Rub this mixture onto the meat, except for the skin.

5. In a bowl, mix the remaining 1 teaspoon of salt and the vinegar.

6. Line a baking sheet with aluminum foil. Place the meat in the center of the foil, skin-side up. Fold the foil up around the meat to cover, leaving the edges ½ inch higher than the meat. Pat the skin dry one more time. Brush the skin with the salt and vinegar mixture.

7. Cover the pork skin completely with an even layer of salt.

8. Bake for 25 minutes. Remove the baking pan from the oven. Turn on the broiler.

9. Unwrap the foil and scrape off the salt layer. Broil until the skin is golden brown, 15 to 20 minutes. Keep an eye after 10 minutes, because the meat might burn faster in smaller ovens.

10. Remove the pan from the oven and let the meat sit for 15 minutes before cutting it into strips along the previous cut lines. Cut each strip into bite-size pieces.

11. In a bowl, combine the rice vermicelli, meat, and chopped herbs. Drizzle with the sauce. Stir to mix and serve.

Variation tip: *This pork can be served on its own over steamed rice or as bánh mì filling.*

Cooking tip: *When shopping, try to choose a piece of meat that is of even thickness. If that's not available, fold a piece of foil and place it under the thinner part to level out the meat. This prevents the skin on the thicker part from burning when the rest is not yet cooked.*

Pan-Seared Duck Breast BÚn Salad *Bún Vịt Áp Chảo*

SERVES 1 • PREP TIME: 10 MINUTES • COOK TIME: 10 MINUTES

*Duck is very popular in Vietnam, especially in the North. The numerous canals, ponds, and rice paddies make this region a paradise for ducks. My father and uncles spent their childhood years herding large flocks of ducks for their parents. Because of the abundance of free-range ducks, street food dishes include duck porridge, noodle soup, and hotpot, plus grilled and pan-seared duck. This dish is inspired by a signature dish at my friend Sơn's restaurant (see **here**). I like that it's tasty and quick, and I don't have to buy a whole duck for a delicious duck plate.*

1 duck breast

Pinch salt

Pinch freshly ground black pepper

1 tablespoon minced ginger

1 tablespoon minced garlic

1½ tablespoons soy sauce

1 tablespoon honey

½ teaspoon minced hot chile or red pepper flakes

2½ ounces rice vermicelli, cooked according to package instructions (or see here)

½ cup fresh Thai/Asian basil leaves or mint leaves

1. Pat the duck breast with a paper towel to make sure it's thoroughly dry. Score the fat almost to the meat.

2. Preheat a sauté pan over high heat for 1 minute. Reduce the heat to medium and place the duck breast, skin-side down, in the pan. Sprinkle with the salt and pepper and cook for 4 minutes. Increase the heat to high and cook until the skin is golden brown and crispy, 1 to 2 minutes. Reduce the heat to low and flip the duck. Fry for 5 minutes for medium rare meat or up to 8 to 10 minutes if you it like well done. Transfer the duck breast to a cutting board, skin-side up; reserve the duck fat in the pan. Let sit for about 5 minutes before slicing to your desired thickness.

3. While waiting for the duck to cool, pour out all but 2 tablespoons of the duck fat and heat the sauté pan over medium heat. Add the ginger and garlic and stir-fry until it starts to brown and release fragrance, about a minute. Reduce the heat to low. Add the soy sauce, honey, and chile, stirring well to combine the sauce.

4. On a plate, mound the rice vermicelli, duck, and herbs. Drizzle with the sauce and serve.

> **Cooking tip:** *The remaining duck fat can be reserved for later use. It's very tasty in sautéed and stir-fried vegetable dishes.*

Stir-Fried Green Beans with Garlic

Braised Baby Back Ribs

Chapter Eight

Cơm
RICE

Sweet and Sour Fish Soup with Tamarind, Pineapple, Tomato Stock, and Mixed Vegetables   *Canh Chua Cá Miền Nam*

Butternut Squash and Ground Pork Soup   *Canh Bí Đỏ it Bằm*

Stir-Fried Beef, Broccoli, and Cauliflower   *it Bò Xào Súp-Lơ*

Stir-Fried Green Beans with Garlic   *Đậu (Đỗ) Xanh/ Đậu Cô-Ve Xào Tỏi*

Fried Tofu Braised in Tomato Sauce   *Đậu Phu Sốt Cà Chua*

Shrimp in Tangy and Sweet Tamarind Sauce   *Tôm Rang Me*

Braised Baby Back Ribs   *Sườn Ram*

Southern Chicken Wings   *Cánh Gà Chiên Nước Mắm*

Braised Pork and Egg in Caramel Sauce and Coconut Water *it Kho Trứng*

Braised Chicken in Lemongrass and Ginger Caramel Sauce *Gà Kho Gừng Xả*

Braised Mushroom and Tofu in Caramel Soy Sauce *Đậu Phụ Kho Nấm*

Salmon in Black Pepper and Caramel Glaze *Cá Hồi Sốt Tiêu Đen*

As mentioned in the introduction, Vietnamese culture values rice so highly that the word itself refers both to the grain and generally to any meal that includes rice, like protein dishes, vegetables, and soups. When people in Vietnam greet each other with the question, "Have you eaten rice yet?" it really means, "Did you eat yet?" This chapter covers "rice" in the sense of a typical Vietnamese meal; in other words, dishes served with steamed rice. I'll be referring to these dishes as cơm.

Cơm doesn't come to mind as street food because it's what we eat every day at home—a staple food for busy families. However, rice vendors (*quán cơm*) in marketplaces and on the street outnumber those hawking noodles and bánh. Noodles and bánh are delicious, but they're considered snacks or a light meal. Cơm, on the other hand, is popular for lunch when we need energy. The Vietnmese believe you have to eat rice to be strong, because it's what we were taught from an early age at home and in school.

On the street, a typical rice vendor displays trays of meat, fish, tofu, eggs, vegetables, and soup. Diners usually order one or two main dishes and the seller arranges them on a platter with rice. Cơm dishes are often not as labor-intensive or complicated as some noodles and bánh. In fact, many are simple and quick enough to cook every day and even twice a day for some families.

This chapter presents our classic cơm food, including soups (canh), stir-fried dishes (xào), and braised dishes (kho). If you try the dishes in this chapter, you'll be eating the same kind of food that the Queen of Denmark ate when she was in Vietnam (see sidebar below). Also, when it comes to cơm, there is no standard or "correct" recipe. For the Vietnamese, the best cơm is always one cooked by their mother, their grandmother, or other relative. Ask any Vietnamese to rate a recipe, and most will fault it because it does not include some favorite family ingredient, or because it includes one they believe should not be there! These recipes are from my grandmother, my aunts, my mother, and also from my friends and their mothers. All the food in this chapter is traditionally served over steamed rice. However, most of these dishes can be eaten on their own or served with a simple salad if you're following a low-carb diet.

Fit For a Queen

In 2009, while working as an interpreter for the Danish Royal delegation to Vietnam, I had the opportunity to attend state banquets hosted in Hanoi, Hue, and Saigon — three major cities representing three different regions. I had been very curious about what food would be offered to the queen, and was excited to learn that it was cơm accompanied by everyday dishes like braised fish in caramel sauce, stir-fried water spinach, and sweet and sour fish soup. We confidently offered the queen dishes from traditional Vietnamese home cooking, one of the most important sources of our national pride. We gave her the foods that we would dearly miss if we were away from home. They're simple but unique foods; and if done well, they can be every bit as good as the fancy royal treats she is probably used to.

Sweet and Sour Fish Soup With Tamarind, Pineapple, Tomato Stock, and Mixed Vegetables *Canh Chua Cá ền Nam*

SERVES 2 OR 3 • PREP TIME: 15 MINUTES • COOK TIME: 15 MINUTES

My two aunts have been living in the south of Vietnam for almost three decades and they're still not fans of southern food, saying it's a little too sweet for them. However, they're diehard fans of this soup and they converted me as well. This is one that I would proudly introduce to Vietnamese food newbies. It includes everything that makes Vietnamese food special: perfectly balanced sweet, sour, salty, and spicy flavors; vegetables and fruits with a refreshing tropical taste; and an amazing aroma from chopped fresh herbs. Every time I eat this dish, I shamelessly ask for more, even after several bowls.

2 tablespoons tamarind paste

⅓ cup boiling water

3 tablespoons vegetable oil

1 tablespoon minced garlic

1 cup thin pineapple slices

1 cup thin tomato wedges

½ teaspoon minced fresh hot chile, plus more if necessary

2 tablespoons sugar

3 cups room-temperature water

1 pound fish fillet or fish steak

5 okra, cut diagonally into thin slices

½ cup bean sprouts (optional)

1 taro root or celery stalk, peeled and cut diagonally into thin slices (optional)

Salt or fish sauce

½ cup fresh rice paddy herb or cilantro, chopped

Steamed rice, for serving (optional)

1. In a small bowl, mix the tamarind paste and boiling water. Break the paste apart with a spoon and let sit for 15 minutes. Mash the paste and water mixture until it becomes fine and smooth. Strain the mixture through a fine-mesh strainer into another bowl and discard the seeds. Set aside.

2. Heat the oil in a saucepan over medium heat. Add the garlic and sauté until fragrant, about 30 seconds. Add the pineapple, tomato, hot chile, and sugar. Stir-fry for 1 minute. Add the room-temperature water and the tamarind mixture. Cover and bring to a boil over medium heat.

3. Add the fish, okra, bean sprouts, and taro (if using). Cover and return to a boil. Season with salt or fish sauce. Turn off the heat. Stir in the rice paddy herb.

4. Serve immediately, with steamed rice or on its own. If you serve with steamed rice, ladle the soup over the steamed rice in each bowl. The soup should cover the rice. Stir to mix and serve.

Variation tip: This recipe also works with shrimp. To make it vegan, substitute mushrooms or simply omit the fish.

Cooking tip: Traditionally, we don't cut the fish into smaller pieces before serving. Instead, we break off pieces with chopsticks as we're eating. However, you can cut it into bite-size pieces to make it easier to share or handle.

Butternut Squash and Ground Pork Soup *Canh Bí Đỏ Thịt Bằm*

SERVES 4 • PREP TIME: 10 MINUTES • COOK TIME: 20 MINUTES

This dish is not as glamorous and elaborate as the Sweet and Sour Fish Soup, but it's delicious in a simple, satisfying, and comforting way. This soup has a deep umami flavor from slow-cooked ground pork, sautéed shallots, and butternut squash cubes. The fresh herbs add another layer of exciting tastes and fragrances for the senses.

8 ounces ground pork

2 tablespoons minced shallot, divided

1 teaspoon salt

Pinch freshly ground black pepper

2 tablespoons vegetable oil

4 cups water

1 pound butternut squash, peeled, seeded, and cut into cubes

Salt or fish sauce

½ cup fresh cilantro leaves, basil, or saw-tooth herb leaves, chopped

Steamed rice, for serving (optional)

1. In a bowl, combine the ground pork with 1 tablespoon of shallot, the salt, and the pepper.

2. Heat the oil in a medium saucepan over medium heat. Add the remaining 1 tablespoon of shallot and sauté until fragrant, about 1 minute. Add the ground pork and stir-fry for 1 minute. Add the water. Cover and bring to a boil, then

reduce the heat to low. Skim off any foam with a fine-mesh skimmer. Add the butternut squash and cook until the squash is soft, 15 to 20 minutes. Turn off the heat. Season the soup with salt or fish sauce and scatter the chopped herbs on top.

3. Serve immediately, with steamed rice or on its own. If you serve it with steamed rice, ladle the soup over the steamed rice in each bowl. The soup should cover the rice. Stir to mix and serve.

Substitution tip: You can substitute coarsely chopped shrimp for the pork in this recipe. If you want to make it vegan, substitute coarsely chopped raw peanuts. In fact, the shrimp and peanut versions of this soup are as popular in Vietnam as the pork version.

Stir-Fried Beef, Broccoli, and Cauliflower *Thịt Bò Xào Súp-Lơ*

SERVES 2 OR 3 • PREP TIME: 15 MINUTES • COOK TIME: 15 MINUTES

Cauliflower, brought to Vietnam by the French, still has a French name, súp-lơ, derived from the French word chou-fleur. *When I was small, we ate súp-lơ as a special luxury during spring holidays, when it was in season. Broccoli is also called súp-lơ because of its similarity in shape to cauliflower. Now that people have become more prosperous in Vietnam, we don't have to wait for special occasions. The beef is cut into thin slices so it's very tender and soaks up all the marinade. The crunchy vegetables are stir-fried in oil and garlic, and they absorb the flavorful meat juices.*

- 8 ounces beef tenderloin, very thinly sliced against the grain
- 3 tablespoons soy sauce
- 8 tablespoons vegetable oil, divided
- 2 teaspoons sugar
- Freshly ground black pepper
- 1 tablespoon salt, plus more if necessary
- 1 cup broccoli florets
- 1 cup cauliflower florets
- 3 tablespoons minced garlic, divided
- Steamed rice, for serving (optional)

1. In a large bowl, toss the beef slices with the soy sauce, 2 tablespoons of oil, the sugar, and season with pepper. Set aside.

2. Fill a large saucepan with water. Add the salt and stir until it dissolves. Bring the water to a boil over high heat. Add the broccoli and cauliflower and blanch for 1 minute. Drain the vegetables in a colander.

3. Heat a sauté pan over high heat. Swirl in 2 tablespoons of oil to spread it evenly. Add 1½ tablespoons of garlic and sauté until fragrant, about 1 minute. Add the beef and stir-fry for almost a minute. The beef should be medium rare. Transfer the beef to a bowl or plate.

4. In the same sauté pan, swirl in the remaining 4 tablespoons of oil to spread it evenly. Add the remaining 1½ tablespoons of garlic and sauté until fragrant, about 1 minute. Add the broccoli and cauliflower and stir-fry for 2 minutes. Season with salt and stir-fry for about 3 minutes, depending on the desired softness. Return the beef to the pan, toss with the vegetables, and stir-fry for 1 minute. Remove from the heat. Sprinkle with freshly ground black pepper. Serve immediately with steamed rice or on its own.

Variation tip: This recipe also works with other vegetables, such as sugar snap peas, bok choy, and zucchini.

Cooking tip: Chill the beef in the freezer for 45 minutes to 1 hour before slicing. This makes it easier to cut into very thin slices.

Stir-Fried Green Beans With Garlic *Đậu (Đỗ) Xanh / Đậu Cô-Ve Xào Tỏi*

SERVES 2 • PREP TIME: 15 MINUTES • COOK TIME: 7 MINUTES

*Green beans were also brought to Vietnam by the French, as was the technique for cutting them. By cutting bean pods à la française — diagonally into thin slices — they look pretty and cook fast, resulting in a perfect crunch while coaxing out the natural sweetness of the beans. I've been cutting beans this way since I was five years old, so if a little kid can get it, you certainly can, too! An alternative way to stir-fry beans is to blanch them in boiling water and then stir-fry the same way you stir-fry the broccoli in **Stir-Fried Beef, Broccoli, and Cauliflower**.*

1 pound green beans

¼ cup vegetable oil

2 tablespoons minced garlic

Salt

Steamed rice, for serving (optional)

1. Trim the stem ends from the beans and remove the strings. Cut the beans diagonally into thin slices, or break the beans in half crosswise and then cut in half lengthwise.
2. Heat the oil in a sauté pan over high heat. Add the garlic and sauté until fragrant, about 1 minute. Add the beans and stir-fry for 2 minutes. Season with salt. Toss for 2 more minutes for crunchy beans, or 4 more minutes if you want them softer.
3. Remove from the heat, and serve with steamed rice or on their own.

Variation tip: *Stir-fry the beans with a small amount of shredded carrot to make the dish more colorful.*

Our Daily Tofu Hawker

When I was growing up, each morning at 6:30 a tofu hawker would walk by our front yard, where I was waiting with a plate and a paper note my mom gave me before leaving for work. The hawker would carefully unveil a thin cloth cover and transfer the warm tofu bars from her bamboo basket onto my plate. The tofu was still steaming and smelled like fresh soy milk. In the late

afternoon, I would fry them in preparation for dinner. My family rarely ate tofu raw and plain. We preferred to fry and dip it in scallion fish sauce. When tomatoes were in season, I would braise the tofu in fresh homemade tomato sauce. Đậu Phụ Sốt Cà Chua (see here) exemplifies the depth and deliciousness of tofu prepared just right.

Fried Tofu Braised In Tomato Sauce *Đậu Phụ Sốt Cà Chua*

SERVES 2 • PREP TIME: 5 MINUTES • COOK TIME: 20 MINUTES

My family used to eat tofu almost every day, and this dish is still one of my favorites. Simple as it may sound, it's one of the best loved classic Vietnamese dishes. The tofu is fried until golden and crispy on the outside but still tender on the inside. Then it's braised in a sweet, rich, creamy fresh tomato sauce made with chopped scallions for fragrance and color. It's a light but truly satisfying northern Vietnamese dish.

1 (10-ounce) block firm tofu

¼ cup vegetable oil

3 scallions, chopped, white and green parts separated

2 medium or 3 small tomatoes, cut into thin wedges

1½ teaspoons salt, plus more if necessary

Steamed rice, for serving

1. Pat the tofu with a paper towel, the drier, the better to reduce spattering when frying. Cut the tofu into ½-inch pieces.

2. Heat a medium sauté pan over medium-high heat. Swirl in the oil to spread it evenly. Add the tofu and fry until golden on the bottom, about 7 minutes. Flip and fry the other side until golden, about 5 minutes. Transfer the tofu to a plate.

3. Lower the heat to medium. Add the white parts of the scallions to the oil remaining in the pan and sauté until soft and fragrant, about 1 minute. Add the tomatoes and salt and stir-fry until the tomatoes are mashed and become a paste,

3 to 5 minutes. Season with more salt, making it slightly salty so it balances out when the tofu is added.

4. Add the tofu and cook for about 7 minutes, lightly tossing occasionally so the tomato sauce coats the tofu evenly. Add the green parts of the scallions and lightly toss to mix.

5. Serve with steamed rice.

Ingredient tip: You can use any tomatoes for this recipe, but the best ones are beefsteak tomatoes because they're sweeter and less watery than other kinds.

Shrimp In Tangy and Sweet Tamarind Sauce
Tôm Rang

SERVES 2 • PREP TIME: 7 MINUTES • COOK TIME: 10 MINUTES

This southern dish uses tamarind to create a distinctive sweet and sour glaze that pairs beautifully with shrimp. Tamarind is a tropical fruit that looks like a big peanut in the shell. The fruit is removed and seeded and creates a paste that is very tart and fresh tasting. This dish has layers of aroma — sautéed garlic, tangy tamarind, and chopped fresh cilantro. It is delicious over steamed rice, which helps moderate the tartness, but you can also eat it with a salad of cucumber, lettuce, and tomatoes.

1 pound large shrimp, peeled and deveined

1 teaspoon salt

2 teaspoons freshly ground black pepper, divided

2 tablespoons tamarind paste

½ cup boiling water

2 tablespoons fish sauce or soy sauce

3 tablespoons sugar

¼ cup vegetable oil

3 tablespoons minced garlic

3 scallions, chopped

½ cup fresh cilantro leaves, chopped

Steamed rice, for serving

1. In a large bowl, season the shrimp with the salt and 1 teaspoon of pepper. Set aside.

2. In a small bowl, mix the tamarind paste and boiling water. Break the paste apart with a spoon and let sit for 15 minutes. Mash the paste and water mixture until it becomes fine and smooth. Strain the mixture through a fine-mesh strainer into another bowl and discard the seeds. Add the fish sauce, sugar, and remaining 1 teaspoon of pepper. Stir well to combine and set aside.

3. In a sauté pan over high heat, heat the oil. Add the garlic and sauté until fragrant and lightly brown, about 1 minute. Add the shrimp and stir-fry 1 to 2 minutes, until the shrimp are pink. Add the tamarind mixture. Cook, stirring occasionally, until the sauce is reduced by half. Remove the pan from the heat.

4. Add the scallions and cilantro. Serve with steamed rice.

***Cooking tip:** To make it spicy, add red pepper flakes or minced fresh hot chiles to the tamarind mixture.*

Braised Baby Back Ribs *Sườn Ram*

SERVES 4 • PREP TIME: 5 MINUTES • COOK TIME: 50 MINUTES

I learned this dish from my friend Sa, a native of the central region who went to school with me in New York. While studying at Columbia's Teachers College, we stayed in the same dorm and would get together on weekends to make Vietnamese dinners like this one in the tiny dorm kitchen. We must have really been craving some home-style food to brave cooking in that cramped space! These ribs are worth the effort — tender and flavorful with a peppery fish sauce glaze. This dish can be served with steamed rice or with pickles or simple salads.

1 tablespoon salt

2 pounds baby back ribs, cut into 1½-inch pieces

¼ cup fish sauce or soy sauce

3 tablespoons sugar

1½ teaspoons freshly ground black pepper

2 tablespoons minced garlic, divided

2 tablespoons minced shallot, divided

2 tablespoons vegetable oil

1½ cups fresh or canned coconut juice or water

Steamed rice, for serving

1. Fill a large saucepan with water and add the salt. Stir well and bring to a boil over high heat. Add the ribs and return to a boil. Turn off the heat. Drain the ribs and rinse under running water. Drain again. Rinse the saucepan.

2. In a large bowl, toss the ribs with the fish sauce, sugar, pepper, 1 tablespoon of garlic, and 1 tablespoon of shallot. Set aside to marinate for 15 minutes.

3. In the same saucepan, heat the oil over medium heat. Add the remaining 1 tablespoon of garlic and 1 tablespoon of shallot and sauté until fragrant, about 30 seconds. Add the marinated ribs and stir-fry for 2 minutes. Add the coconut juice and stir to combine. Reduce the heat to low and cook for about 40 minutes, stirring occasionally.

4. Increase the heat to medium-high. Stir constantly until the sauce starts to caramelize and coat the ribs evenly, 2 to 3 minutes.

5. Serve with steamed rice.

Cooking tip: *These ribs can be served on their own and go great with a cold beer. If you don't plan on serving the ribs with rice, reduce the fish sauce or soy sauce to 2½ tablespoons.*

Southern Chicken Wings *Cánh Gà Chiên Nước Mắm*

SERVES 2 OR 3 • PREP TIME: 10 MINUTES • COOK TIME: 15 MINUTES

These golden-fried wings coated in a sweet, sour, spicy, and salty garlic chili sauce will have you cleaning them off the bone! When we lived in New York and my husband invited his friends over, this was one of my go-to meals — so easy to prepare and such a crowd pleaser! Fish sauce adds an interesting umami depth, and garlic offers another layer of taste and texture. Perfect for gatherings — and a great beer food — it can also simply be served over steamed rice.

3 tablespoons fish sauce

2½ tablespoons rice vinegar or apple cider vinegar

2 tablespoons water

3 tablespoons sugar

1 tablespoon minced fresh hot chile (optional)

1½ pound chicken wings

5 tablespoons vegetable oil

3 tablespoons minced garlic

Steamed rice, for serving (optional)

1. In a bowl, whisk the fish sauce, vinegar, water, sugar, and hot chile (if using) until the sugar dissolves. Add more fish sauce, vinegar, and sugar if necessary. Set aside.

2. Wash the wings and drain well. Cut each wing at the joint, discarding the wing tip. Pat the wings dry with a paper towel, the drier, the better to reduce spattering when frying.

3. In a sauté pan over high heat, heat the oil for 1 minute. Reduce the heat to medium. Add the wings and fry until golden on one side, about 10 minutes. Turn and fry until the other side is golden, 8 to 10 minutes. Transfer the chicken wings to paper towels to drain.
4. Pour the excess oil from the pan into a bowl for later use, reserving about 1 tablespoon in the pan. Heat the pan over medium heat. Add the garlic and sauté until fragrant and golden, about 1 minute. Add the sauce and the chicken wings. Toss the wings constantly until the sauce is reduced and the wings are evenly coated in a golden sticky glaze.
5. Serve the wings on their own or over steamed rice.

Cooking tip: *Partially cover the pan when frying to prevent spattering oil.*

Braised Pork and Egg in Caramel Sauce and Coconut Water *Thịt Kho Trứng*

SERVES 6 • PREP TIME: 5 MINUTES • COOK TIME: 2 HOURS 30 MINUTES

This is a somewhat elaborate braised dish, but it's meant to be stretched over two or more meals, and most of the cook time is passive. My husband lists this as one of his favorite meals, and I used to pack it for him when he was working at a hospital in New York. He had co-workers in his office, a Cambodian-American and a Filipino-American, whose cultures also treasure this dish, so they were always envious when he brought it! Pork belly or pork shoulder is slow-cooked in coconut water until the meat is rich and tender, and the fat melts in your mouth. Northerners might add quail eggs, while southerners prefer duck eggs for this dish. I opt for chicken eggs.

3 tablespoons sugar

3 tablespoons room-temperature water

¼ cup boiling water

1 teaspoon salt

2 pounds pork belly or pork shoulder

5 tablespoons fish sauce

1 head garlic, cloves peeled

Fresh hot chiles, sliced (optional)

3½ cups coconut water

6 hardboiled eggs, peeled (optional)

Steamed rice, for serving

1. In a saucepan or sauté pan, combine the sugar and room-temperature water without stirring. Cook over medium-high heat until the sugar starts to turn honey colored. Swirl the pan to distribute the heat and the sugar evenly. When the sugar is consistently honey colored, reduce the heat to low.

2. Very carefully ladle the boiling water over the caramelized sugar. Stir constantly until the crystallized caramelized sugar is fully dissolved in water, then turn off the heat. Transfer the caramel sauce to a bowl and set aside.

3. Fill a saucepan with enough water to cover the pork. Add the salt and bring to a boil over medium-high heat. Gently add the pork to the boiling water. Cover and return to a boil. Drain the pork and rinse under running water. Drain again. Pat the pork dry with a paper towel and cut it into ½-inch-thick slices. Each piece should have three layers—skin, fat, and lean meat. Rinse the saucepan.

4. In the same saucepan, combine the pork, caramel sauce, fish sauce, garlic, and chiles (if using). Mix well and pour the coconut water over the meat. Stir gently, cover, and bring to a boil over medium-high heat. Turn down the heat to low and skim off any foam with a fine-mesh skimmer. Add the hardboiled eggs (if using). Cover and cook over low heat for 2 hours, stirring occasionally. After 2 hours, the stock should be reduced by about half.

5. If desired, uncover, increase the heat to medium-high, and cook until the sauce is reduced and becomes a thick glaze (see cooking tip).

6. To serve, put some pork in each bowl. Halve the eggs and place them over the pork. Drizzle with the caramel sauce. Serve with steamed rice.

Substitution tip: You can use soft-boiled eggs instead of hardboiled eggs. Add soft-boiled eggs to the pot after braising the pork for 2 hours, and after the optional reduction. The eggs should be in the pot for 1 to 2 minutes, just long enough for the sauce to coat them. Use chopsticks or a spoon or spatula to roll the eggs so the sauce coats them evenly.

Variation tip: The caramel sauce can be used to marinate barbecue meat as in Grilled Pork Bún with Herbs and Sweet and Sour Dipping Sauce. This sauce makes the meat tender and adds depth of flavor and color.

Cooking tip: *The reduction in step 5 is optional. I like the glaze to be thick and have a buttery texture reminiscent of the northern style, but many people like to have more stock like a southern-style soup bowl.*

Braised Chicken in Lemongrass and Ginger Caramel Sauce
Gà Kho Gừng Xả

SERVES 2 • PREP TIME: 15 MINUTES • COOK TIME: 15 MINUTES

This is another recipe from my quick-easy-tasty repertoire. The chicken is immersed in an elegant marinade infused with warm spices like ginger, lemongrass, black pepper, and hot chiles. The caramel sauce adds a mild sweetness to contrast the spicy and salty flavors of the chicken. In addition to its big, contrasting flavors, the dish's aroma is knock-you-out amazing — warm, tropical, festive, and absolutely mouthwatering! Use any part of the chicken that you like for this recipe. Traditionally, Vietnamese people prefer bone-in and skin-on chicken whacked into small pieces with a cleaver, but any boneless sliced chicken is fine too.

1 pound chicken parts, cut into ½-inch pieces

5 lemongrass stalks (about 3 inches of the roots only), finely chopped, divided

1 (2-inch) piece ginger, peeled and minced, divided

1 teaspoon minced fresh hot chile (optional)

3 tablespoons fish sauce

Freshly ground black pepper

3 tablespoons sugar

3 tablespoons room-temperature water

¼ cup boiling water

2 tablespoons vegetable oil

Steamed rice, for serving

1. In a large bowl, toss the chicken with half of the lemongrass and half of the ginger, the hot chile (if using), the fish sauce, and season with pepper. Set aside to marinate for 15 minutes.

2. In a saucepan or sauté pan, combine the sugar and room-temperature water without stirring. Cook over medium-high heat until the sugar starts to turn honey colored. Swirl the pan to distribute the heat and the sugar evenly. When the sugar is consistently honey colored, reduce the heat to low.

3. Very carefully ladle the boiling water over the caramelized sugar. Stir constantly until the crystallized caramelized sugar is fully dissolved in the water, then turn off the heat. Transfer to a bowl and set aside.

4. Heat the oil in a saucepan over medium-high heat. Add the remaining lemongrass and ginger and sauté until fragrant, about 1 minute. Add the chicken and sauté for 1 minute. Reduce the heat to medium-low. Add the caramel sauce and stir to mix, then cover and cook for 15 minutes.

5. Serve with steamed rice.

Variation tip: *This recipe also works with fish.*

Ingredient tip: *It's okay to skip the lemongrass if it's not in season or if it's not available. Instead, double the amount of ginger. In fact, braised ginger chicken is another popular dish in Vietnam.*

Braised Mushroom and Tofu in Caramel Soy Sauce *Đậu Phụ Kho Nấm*

SERVES 2 • PREP TIME: 5 MINUTES • COOK TIME: 25 MINUTES

I had this dish at a restaurant that became famous after Brad Pitt and Angelina Jolie ate there many years ago. The menu includes dishes inspired by the owner's grandmother, whose kitchen and garden were on the outskirts of Saigon, so it is an example of southern Vietnamese home cooking at its finest. The savory-sweet black pepper caramel sauce gives the soft tofu and crunchy mushrooms a complex yet light and satisfying flavor.

- 7 ounces enoki mushrooms or clamshell mushrooms (also known as beech or shimeji mushrooms), trimmed of roots
- 3 tablespoons sugar
- 3 tablespoons room-temperature water
- ¼ cup boiling water
- 1 (10-ounce) block firm tofu
- ¼ cup vegetable oil
- 2 tablespoons minced shallot
- ¼ cup soy sauce
- 1 teaspoon minced fresh hot chile or hot chili sauce (optional)
- Freshly ground black pepper
- Steamed rice, for serving

1. In a large bowl, soak the mushrooms in lightly salted water for 10 minutes, then gently rinse with fresh water. Drain well.

2. In a saucepan or sauté pan, combine the sugar and room-temperature water without stirring. Cook over medium-high heat until the sugar starts to turn honey colored. Swirl the pan to distribute the heat and the sugar evenly. When the sugar is consistently honey colored, reduce the heat to low.

3. Very carefully ladle the boiling water over the caramelized sugar. Stir constantly until the caramelized sugar is fully dissolved in the water, then turn off the heat. Transfer to a bowl and set aside.

4. Pat the tofu dry with a paper towel, the drier, the better to reduce spattering when frying. Cut the tofu into ½-inch pieces.

5. Heat a medium sauté pan over medium-high heat. Swirl in the oil to spread it evenly. Add the tofu and fry until golden on the bottom, about 7 minutes. Flip and fry the other side until golden, about 5 minutes. Transfer the tofu to a plate.

6. Add the shallot to the oil remaining in the pan and sauté until fragrant, about 1 minute. Add the mushrooms and tofu. Add the soy sauce, caramel sauce, hot chile (if using), and season with pepper. Stir well to mix. Reduce the heat to low, cover, and cook for 15 minutes.

7. Serve with steamed rice.

Substitution tip: *You can substitute any other mushrooms that you like. However, softer mushrooms will absorb the sauce better.*

Salmon In Black Pepper and Caramel Glaze *Cá Hồi Sốt Tiêu đen*

SERVES 2 • PREP TIME: 5 MINUTES • COOK TIME: 10 MINUTES

This is a variation of Vietnamese braised fish in caramel sauce. As much as I love that dish, it uses small whole fish or fish steaks with bones, which you have to worry about. So I substitute salmon fillet. It's quick to make and absolutely delicious. Black pepper, soy sauce, and caramel sauce enhance the salmon, making it a perfect dish to pair with steamed rice.

3 tablespoons sugar

¼ cup room-temperature water

⅓ cup boiling water

3 tablespoons fish sauce or soy sauce

1 pound salmon fillet, skinned and cut into ½-inch-thick slices

Freshly ground black pepper

3 tablespoons vegetable oil, divided

Steamed rice, for serving

1. In a saucepan or sauté pan, combine the sugar and room-temperature water without stirring. Cook over medium-high heat until the sugar starts to turn honey colored. Swirl the pan to distribute the heat and the sugar evenly. When the sugar is consistently honey colored, reduce the heat to low.

2. Very carefully ladle the boiling water over the caramelized sugar. Stir constantly until the caramelized sugar is fully dissolved in water. Stir in the fish sauce. Add the salmon. Season with pepper and drizzle half of the oil over the

salmon. Cook for 3 minutes. Flip the salmon. Sprinkle with more pepper and drizzle with the remaining oil. Cook for 3 additional minutes.

3. Serve immediately with steamed rice.

Cooking tip: *Add minced ginger to the sauce to make it even more fragrant.*

Mango Tapioca Pudding

Chapter Nine

Đồ Uống and Món Ngọt
DRINKS AND SWEET TREATS

Vietnamese Coffee *Cà Phê Phin*

Lemongrass Tea *Trà Sả*

Avocado Smoothie *Sinh Tố Bơ*

Calamondin / Kumquat Refresher *Nước Quất Mật Ong*

Crème Caramel *Ca-ra-men/Bánh Flan*

Sesame Rice Doughnuts *Bánh Rán Vừng*

Vietnamese Mochi in Sweet Ginger Water and Coconut Milk *Chè Trôi Nước/Bánh Trôi Tàu*

Banana Tapioca Pudding in Coconut Milk *Chè Chuối*

Mango Tapioca Pudding *Chè Xoài*

Areca Blossom Pudding *Chè Hoa Cau*

Soy Pudding in Ginger Syrup *Tào Phớ*

Crispy Banana Fritters *Chuối Chiên*

Panna Cotta with Fresh Passion Fruit Juice *Panna Cotta Chanh Dây*

Because of the abundance of fresh fruit in Vietnam, we usually enjoy our fruit drinks in their freshest form, meaning plucked right off the branch and squeezed into a drinking glass on the same day. Fresh coconut juice and fresh sugar cane juice are among the most common drinks—you can find them almost anywhere, from a deserted beach to a small local market or a buzzing urban street. Locals and tourists alike enjoy seeing a vendor chop off the end of a young coconut and simply stick a straw into it, or feeding sugar cane into a machine that looks like an old-fashioned clothes wringer but spills marvelously fresh sugar cane juice into your glass.

When we make and mix our drinks, we tend to focus on the medicinal values of the ingredients. Our fragrant herbal drinks usually function as a remedy of some sort, although the goal might be as simple as cooling down or warming up your body.

Our most common and favorite dessert is not covered in this book, nor probably in any other authentic cookbook: It's simply fresh fruit. After lunch or dinner, the woman of the house presents a platter of cut-up fruit for the whole family to share. This simple act demonstrates her care for her family and provides a nice social time after a meal.

Besides fresh fruit, we also love rice-based sweet treats (bánh) and slow-cooked pudding-like desserts (chè), but we usually eat those on the streets or at local markets. We make them at home only on weekends or for special occasions. The most popular street-bought sweet treat that you'll find throughout the country is chè, which is made by slow-cooking different kinds of grains or fruits in sugar water or coconut milk, served cold with crushed ice in the summer and warm in the winter. It has a puddinglike texture but is a bit more watery, so chè to us is both a dessert and a drink. We eat the fruits or beans and then drink the refreshing water in between bites. Many westerners are surprised to see beans as a dessert, but you'd be surprised at how well the earthy flavors and textures of cooked beans pair with the sweetness and smoothness of chè and jelly. Northern chè is light and delicate, with naturally infused floral scents from jasmine flowers or pomelo blossoms. By contrast, southern chè involves rich, creamy, complex flavors and textures from coconut cream, tapioca, and roasted seeds and nuts.

Besides traditional Vietnamese desserts, there are desserts with French and Chinese influences. You'll find those foreign-influenced recipes in this chapter alongside our home-grown sweet treats.

The Ceremony Of Coffee

Like many cultures around the world, in Vietnam we take coffee, or cà phê as we call it, seriously. If you want to ask somebody to hang out or meet up, you say "Would you like to cà phê tonight?" Traditional Vietnamese coffee is brewed in a small filter kit the size of a tea cup, which sits on top of the coffee cup dripping rich, aromatic coffee drop by drop. It's called "cà phê phin," with phin *being the Vietnamese word for "filter." Cà phê phin time is usually reserved for quality time with friends when you are not in a hurry and don't mind waiting for the coffee to drip. This is a good drink to test your company's patience — hence, an ideal drink to order on a first date! On Vietnamese New Year, we might wish somebody good fortune by saying, "I hope this year your money will flow in as quickly as a river and flow out as slowly as from a phin." Some people prefer their coffee either over ice (đá) or hot (nóng), but it is delicious either way.*

Vietnamese Coffee *Cà Phê Phin*

SERVES 1 • PREP TIME: 2 MINUTES • BREWING TIME: 15 MINUTES

Vietnamese coffee is brewed from Robusta beans, while most of the world has moved on to Arabica beans. If brewed correctly, Robusta beans can make a terrific pot of coffee that is good with a bit of sweetened condensed milk or served đen, or dark. My husband, who found Robusta to be pretty tasteless in the United States, was surprised to drink really fresh and delicious Robusta in Vietnam. If you can't find high-quality, fresh Robusta coffee, a good substitute is Café Du Monde from New Orleans, which was available at every small grocery in New York when I lived there. You'll also need a Vietnamese coffee filter kit, which you can find on Amazon.

1½ tablespoons condensed milk, plus more if necessary

2 tablespoons ground coffee

Boiling water

3 to 5 small ice cubes

1. Pour the condensed milk into a cup or mug. Place the filter on top of the cup. Add the coffee and lightly shake to spread the coffee evenly. Gently press and twist the filter press clockwise — don't twist too tightly or the water won't drip through.
2. Add about 1½ tablespoons of boiling water. Put on the cap and let sit for about 2 minutes.
3. Remove the cap and slowly pour boiling water into the filter to almost full. Replace the cap and wait until all the water drips through the filter, about 15 minutes.

4. Stir well to dissolve the condensed milk. Add the ice cubes, stir well, and serve.

> **Cooking tip:** If you want to serve this coffee hot, rinse the cup and filter in boiling water before making the coffee. Also, place the cup in a bowl of boiling water while waiting for the coffee to drip.

Lemongrass Tea _Trà Sả_

SERVES 1 • PREP TIME: 2 MINUTES • COOK TIME: 10 MINUTES

Like many rural Vietnamese women, my grandmother and aunts would always start their morning by brewing a big pot of green or seasonal herbal tea for the family to drink throughout the day. During the warmer months, when the lemongrass bushes grew like weeds, we had more than enough lemongrass to eat, give away, and sell, so my grandmother would brew lemongrass tea. The whole house was flooded with the pleasant and therapeutic aroma of lemongrass. According to Vietnamese traditional medicine, lemongrass aids digestion and improves liver function. Condensed or thickened lemongrass juice is a great traditional hangover remedy. I enjoy my lemongrass tea plain, but you can add honey if you'd like. This tea smells heavenly and leaves a pleasant tingle in your mouth.

10 lemongrass stalks

1½ cups water

Honey (optional)

1. Peel off any old or dry outer leaves from the lemongrass. Trim the leaves, keeping about 3 inches of the roots. With the back of a big knife, pestle, or meat hammer, crush the lemongrass stalks to release their fragrance.
2. In a saucepan, combine the lemongrass stalks and water. Bring to a boil over low heat, about 10 minutes. Turn off the heat and let steep for 10 to 15 minutes.
3. Pour into cups and serve plain or with honey, if desired.

Variation tip: *Some people like to add a few slices of ginger, lemongrass's best friend, for an extra kick of spiciness and fragrance.*

Avocado Smoothie

Tố Bơ

SERVES 1 • PREP TIME: 5 MINUTES

In Vietnam, avocado has always been exclusively eaten for dessert — the avocado smoothie in particular. Avocado smoothie is a popular favorite drink throughout the country, both in smoothie stalls on the streets and in fancy restaurants. My aunts adore avocado season because they can help my skinny cousins gain a few pounds from drinking avocado smoothies every day.

1 ripe Hass avocado, halved and pitted

⅓ cup milk

2 tablespoons condensed milk

3 to 5 small ice cubes

Scoop the avocado flesh into a blender. Add the milk, condensed milk, and ice. Blend until smooth. Pour into a glass and serve.

> **Variation tip:** Substitute honey for the condensed milk and coconut milk for the milk to make the smoothie dairy-free.
>
> **Cooking tip:** You can also mash the avocado, milk, and condensed milk with a spoon until the mixture becomes smooth and then add crushed ice before serving.

Calamondin / Kumquat Refresher
Nước Quất Mật Ong

SERVES 1 • PREP TIME: 5 MINUTES

The Vietnamese word for kumquat is the last syllable of the English word — quất. During Vietnamese New Year, kumquat trees in the north of the country are as festively symbolic as Christmas trees in the West. During the holidays, Vietnamese families invariably decorate their living room with a kumquat tree heavy with yellow fruits, a symbol of good fortune and joy, and it's one of the five fruits we offer in the fruit tray on the family altar during special occasions. We use it to make jam, candy, syrup, dipping sauce, and simple fruit drinks like this one. A rich source of vitamin C and a good cough remedy, this kumquat and honey drink was what my mother and grandmother made for me every morning during the cold season.

5 kumquats, halved crosswise

2 tablespoons honey

¼ cup lukewarm water

1. Squeeze the juice from the kumquats and set aside. In a small bowl, mash the kumquat skin with a spoon to release the oils.
2. In a mug or cup, combine the mashed kumquat skin, kumquat juice, honey, and water.
3. Mix well and serve.

Ingredient tip: *There are different varieties of kumquats, but the ideal kumquat for this recipe is the calamondin. Calamondins look just like* *kumquats or tiny clementines, but they're round and have a shiny thin skin that you can peel easily. This variety of kumquat is much juicier, and it tastes like a mix of lime and mandarin.*

Crème Caramel *Ca-ra-n/Bánh Flan*

SERVES 4 • PREP TIME: 5 MINUTES • COOK TIME: 35 MINUTES

This is one of the French delicacies left to us from colonial times. Crème caramel, called ca-ra-men in the North and bánh flan in the South, is a popular dessert throughout Vietnam. In Hanoi, it's as popular as frozen yogurt is in America, and there's a whole street in the Old Quarter that specializes in it. Can you imagine savoring a French dessert while sitting on a child-size wooden stool on a narrow, ancient Asian street? Crème caramel is among the simplest desserts, yet so delightfully delicious when I have guests over for meals and just want an easy, tasty treat.

FOR THE CARAMEL

⅓ cup sugar

¼ cup water

FOR THE CUSTARD

4 large eggs

3½ cups milk

2 tablespoons sugar

½ teaspoon vanilla extract

To make the caramel

1. In a small saucepan, combine the sugar and water without stirring. Cook over medium-high heat until the sugar starts to turn honey colored. Swirl the pan to distribute the heat and the sugar evenly.

2. Quickly pour the caramel into four 1-cup ramekins. When pouring, rock the ramekin from side to side to distribute the caramel evenly. Do this quickly,

because caramel hardens very fast.

To make the custard

1. Preheat the oven to 300°F and boil a kettle of water (about 8 cups).
2. Whisk the eggs in a bowl and set aside.
3. In a saucepan, heat the milk to almost boiling, about 175°F. Turn off the heat, add the sugar and vanilla extract, and stir well.
4. Pour the hot milk into the eggs, stirring constantly to prevent the eggs from cooking. Strain the custard mixture 3 times to make it smooth and creamy.
5. Place the ramekins with the caramel in a baking pan and pour the custard mixture into the ramekins. Place the baking pan in the oven. Pour the boiling water into the baking pan around the cups. The water should reach about halfway up the sides. Bake for 30 minutes.
6. Let cool and refrigerate for at least 1 hour before serving.
7. To serve, run a knife around the sides of each ramekin. Quickly invert the ramekin over a plate and shake gently to make the crème caramel fall out easily.

Storage tip: Crème caramel can be kept in the refrigerator for up to 5 days. Put plastic wrap over the top to prevent the surface from getting dry.

Sesame Rice Doughnuts *Bánh Rán Vừng*

MAKES ABOUT 20 DOUGHNUTS • PREP TIME: 20 MINUTES + 30 MINUTES TO RISE • COOK TIME: 1 HOUR

These popular snacks are often sold in huge bamboo trays at local markets or carried by women walking from street to street. Emblematic of Asian desserts, it is much less sugary than most Western desserts and incorporates bean paste as the main filling. However, my American husband assures me it's an instantly delicious and enjoyable dessert for a westerner to try.

FOR THE FILLING

¾ cup dry, peeled, split mung beans (also known as yellow beans), soaked in water for 1 to 3 hours and drained

1 cup water

Pinch salt

½ cup sugar

FOR THE DOUGH

2½ cups glutinous rice flour

⅓ cup rice flour

1 cup water

¼ cup sugar

Pinch salt

FOR MAKING THE DOUGHNUTS

1 cup roasted sesame seeds

Vegetable oil, for frying

To make the filling

1. In a saucepan, combine the beans, water, and salt and cook over low heat until soft, about 25 minutes.
2. Add the sugar and stir to mix. Mash the beans using a wooden spoon or a spatula. Increase the heat to medium and stir constantly until a paste forms. Remove the pan from the heat.
3. Once cool enough to handle, form the bean paste into 20 balls.

To make the dough

1. In a large bowl, mix the glutinous rice flour, rice flour, water, sugar, and salt until combined and not sticky.
2. Cover the dough with a slightly damp cloth or plastic wrap and let it rest for 30 minutes.
3. Form the dough into a log and divide into 20 portions. Form each portion into a ball about twice the size of the bean balls.

To make the doughnuts

1. Place a rice ball in the palm of your hand. Flatten it with your fingers. Place a bean ball in the middle, then wrap the rice dough around the bean ball. Make sure it's completely sealed, with no beans showing through. Roll between your palms to form a ball.
2. Dip the ball into a bowl of roasted sesame seeds and roll until fully covered with seeds. Lightly press the seeds into the dough so that they will stick well when frying.
3. Repeat with the remaining rice and bean balls.
4. Pour the vegetable oil into a small saucepan to a depth of 2 inches. Heat over medium heat until the oil reaches 390°F. Test by dipping a chopstick or a fork into the oil. If the oil sizzles, it's ready.
5. Reduce the heat to low. Carefully add some of the doughnuts and fry until they are golden. Using a slotted spoon or strainer, transfer the doughnuts to paper

towels to drain. Repeat with the remaining doughnuts. Serve warm, while the doughnuts are still crispy.

> **Substitution tip:** *You can substitute canned red or black beans for the mung beans.*
>
> **Storage tip:** *These doughnuts are best eaten when freshly made, but you can store them at room temperature for up to 6 hours. They'll get softer over time but will still be delicious.*

Vietnamese Mochi in Sweet Ginger Water and Coconut Milk *Chè Trôi Nước/Bánh Trôi Tàu*

MAKES ABOUT 15 (1½-INCH) BALLS • PREP TIME: 20 MINUTES • COOK TIME: 45 MINUTES

The bean and rice texture of this sweet is similar to that of Japanese mochi, but in Vietnam we call this "floating cake" because it floats when cooked. This is my grandmother's recipe. She used to make this dessert once a year for the traditional "Mochi Day" in early lunar spring. This mochi is drizzled in light ginger syrup and provides a mix of tastes and textures, from the silky coating of rice flour dough to the grainy interior of mung bean paste. Northern Vietnamese eat this with ginger syrup only, but southerners add coconut milk and sesame seeds.

FOR THE MOCHI

¼ cup dry, peeled, split mung beans (also known as yellow beans), soaked in water for 1 to 3 hours and drained

1 cup room-temperature water

Pinch salt

3 tablespoons granulated sugar

2 cups glutinous rice flour

1 cup warm water

FOR THE SYRUP

1 cup palm sugar

2 tablespoons minced ginger

3½ cups water

½ cup roasted sesame seeds (optional)

½ cup coconut milk (optional)

1. In a saucepan, combine the mung beans, room-temperature water, and salt. Cook over medium heat until the beans are soft, about 30 minutes. If the water evaporates before the beans are soft, add a bit more water.

2. Stir in the sugar. Mash the beans. Increase the heat to medium and stir until a paste forms. Remove the pan from the heat.

3. Once cool enough to handle, form the bean paste into 15 balls.

4. In a large bowl, mix the rice flour and warm water until combined, adding a little bit more water or flour to keep it non-sticky.

5. Form the dough into a log and divide into 15 portions. Form each portion into a ball about twice the size of the bean balls.

6. Place a rice ball in the palm of your hand. Flatten it with your fingers. Place a bean ball in the middle, then wrap the rice dough around it until it's completely sealed. Roll between your palms to form a ball. Repeat until all the dough is used. Set the mochi balls on a plate.

7. In a saucepan, combine the palm sugar, ginger, and water. Stir until the sugar dissolves. Bring to a boil over medium heat. Reduce the heat to low. Gently add the mochi and cover. Return to a boil. Uncover periodically to check. When the mochi float, they're done.

8. To serve, place 2 or 3 mochi in each bowl. Pour in the ginger syrup and drizzle with the sesame seeds and coconut milk (if using).

My Grandmother's ChÈ Stall

Chè is such a beloved drink and dessert to me that when I think about it, I can smell the herbal scent of stewed beans and feel the numbness I used to get in my fingers after crushing loads and loads of ice when I helped my grandmother prepare it for her small stall. In Vietnam, there are no gas station rest stops, so travelers stop at small roadside vendors for tea, drinks, chè, and other sweet snacks. My grandmother (not the one I grew up with in the countryside) has been running a beverage and chè stand at the same busy highway intersection for 25 years, and is well known to the people traveling that way on a regular basis. I helped her every day for almost five years while I was in middle school. By "helping," I mean that I watched the stall for her while she was eating lunch in the kitchen, and I helped crush ice, all the while eating as much chè and bánh as I liked as payment for my efforts!

Amazingly, my grandmother is 85 years old now and still running that shop. She is very sharp and never miscalculates when giving change to customers, saying that the secret to her mental sharpness is drinking a lot of the teas that she sells.

Banana Tapioca Pudding In Coconut Milk *Chè Chuối*

SERVES 2 TO 3 • PREP TIME: 5 MINUTES • COOK TIME: 30 MINUTES

In addition to bananas, this dish uses coconut milk, tapioca, and roasted peanuts, three popular ingredients in southern Vietnamese desserts. The ideal bananas for this recipe are the short, chubby ones, also known as bananitos or Thai bananas. They're popular in Chinatown and are also available in well-stocked Western grocery stores. Bananitos are sweeter and firmer than regular bananas, but if you can't find them or if they're not in season, regular bananas work, too. Whichever kind you use, make sure they are ripe or slightly overripe or they'll be tart when cooked.

- ⅔ cup small tapioca pearls (also known as sago), soaked in water for 15 minutes and drained
- 2¼ cups coconut milk
- ¼ cup sugar
- Pinch salt
- 4 short bananas (bananitos or Thai bananas) or 2 regular bananas, peeled and cut crosswise into ½-inch pieces
- ¼ cup roasted peanuts, chopped

1. Bring a small saucepan of water to a boil over medium heat. Add the tapioca. Cook, stirring occasionally, until the tapioca becomes transparent, about 10 minutes. Drain the water and transfer the tapioca to a strainer. Rinse the tapioca under running water until cool. Set aside.

2. In the same saucepan, combine the coconut milk, sugar, and salt and whisk until the sugar dissolves. Add the bananas and bring to a boil over low heat. Add the tapioca and stir to distribute the tapioca evenly. Cover and return to a boil over low heat.

3. To serve, ladle the bananas, tapioca, and coconut milk into small bowls. Sprinkle with roasted peanuts.

Serving tip: This pudding can be served hot or cold. To serve cold, let cool and refrigerate for an hour before serving, or simply add crushed ice if you can't wait.

Ingredient tip: There are different sizes of tapioca. Pick the smallest size, which is often labeled "small pearls." If you don't live near an Asian store, tapioca is available on Amazon.

Mango Tapioca Pudding *Chè Xoài*

SERVES 2 TO 3 • PREP TIME: 10 MINUTES + 2 HOURS TO CHILL • COOK TIME: 15 MINUTES

This is another delicious signature tropical dessert/drink with ripe mangos, coconut cream, condensed milk, and tapioca. Mango cubes and tapioca add contrasting textures, and the coconut and mango flavors blend to make this dessert a perfect summer choice in just a few easy steps. It also has the distinctive tropical aromas of coconut and mango.

3 ripe mangos, peeled, pitted, and cut into cubes

1½ cups coconut milk

¼ cup condensed milk

1 cup small tapioca pearls (also known as sago), soaked in water for 15 minutes and drained

1. In a blender, purée half of the mango cubes with the coconut milk and condensed milk, then put the mixture in the refrigerator. Keep the remaining mango cubes in the refrigerator also.
2. Bring a small saucepan of water to a boil over medium heat. Add the tapioca. Cook, stirring occasionally, until the tapioca becomes transparent, about 10 minutes. Drain the water and transfer the tapioca to a strainer. Rinse the tapioca under running water until cool.
3. Add the tapioca and mango cubes to the mango-coconut mixture. Stir well to mix.
4. Refrigerate for 2 hours before serving.

Substitution tip: *Use sugar instead of condensed milk to make this dessert vegan.*

Cooking tip: *If you don't want to wait for the pudding to chill, add crushed ice or small ice cubes and stir well to mix before serving. Since the ice will dilute the mixture, you'll want to increase the mango amount by half and add more condensed milk.*

Areca Blossom Pudding *Chè H Cau*

MAKES 5 SMALL BOWLS • PREP TIME: 5 MINUTES • COOK TIME: 30 MINUTES

The reasoning for this poetic name is that the yellow beans in this pudding resemble the tiny yellow areca flowers found in the Vietnamese countryside. This pudding also uses arrowroot starch, a thickening powder and wheat substitute believed to have a yin element that cools down the body. In the summer, we mix arrowroot starch with sugar and water to make a quick refreshing drink. My grandmother used to make this pudding because she planted arrowroot vines in her garden. After each crop, she would infuse the starch with pomelo blossoms, also from her garden. Since pomelo blossoms are not available where I live now, I have to make do with vanilla extract to replace that pleasant floral scent that northerners adore.

½ cup dry, peeled, split mung beans (also known as yellow beans), soaked in water for 1 to 3 hours and drained

2¾ cups water, divided

Pinch salt

1 cup palm sugar or ⅔ cup raw sugar

½ cup arrowroot starch

1 teaspoon vanilla extract

1. In a saucepan, combine the beans, ¼ cup of water, and the salt, and cook over medium-low heat until soft, about 20 minutes. Transfer to a bowl and set aside.

2. In the same saucepan, whisk the sugar and 2 cups of water until the sugar dissolves. Bring to a boil over medium heat.

3. Meanwhile, in a bowl, mix the arrowroot starch, vanilla extract, and remaining ½ cup of water. Pour this mixture into the boiling sugar water. Cook over medium heat, whisking constantly, until the mixture thickens and becomes transparent. Add the mung beans and whisk to combine.

4. Ladle the pudding into small bowls. Let cool and serve.

> **Cooking tip:** If you have a rice cooker, throw the beans in the cooker with ¼ cup water and let it do the work.

Soy Pudding In Ginger Syrup *Tào Phớ*

SERVES 10 • PREP TIME: 5 MINUTES + 4 HOURS TO CHILL • COOK TIME: 5 MINUTES

My mother used to reward me with this dessert if I finished my homework early or when she wanted me to be nicer to my little brother. This dessert is sold in local markets, on the streets, and by hawkers biking or walking from street to street. Northerners eat it with light sugar water and virgin jasmine blossom extract. In the central and southern regions, people eat it with palm sugar and ginger syrup. It's always fun to watch vendors serve this pudding. They use a big mother of pearl shell to scrape thin slices of pudding into a bowl, then quickly pour the fragrant syrup over. This silk pudding melts on the tip of your tongue and is so delicious you'll finish your third bowl before you know it.

3¼ cups water, divided

1½ tablespoons powdered gelatin

4¼ cups soy milk

1 cup palm sugar

1 (2-inch) piece ginger, peeled, thinly sliced, and lightly smashed

1. Pour ¼ cup of water into a small bowl. Sprinkle in the powdered gelatin, stirring to break up any clumps.

2. In a saucepan, heat the soy milk over medium heat until hot, but not boiling, about 150°F. Turn off the heat. Add the gelatin mixture to the soy milk and stir well.

3. Transfer the soy milk mixture to a large bowl. Let cool and refrigerate for 4 hours.

4. In the same saucepan, combine the remaining 3 cups of water, the sugar, and ginger, and bring to a boil over medium heat. Turn off the heat. Let cool and refrigerate for 4 hours.

5. To serve, use a broad, flat spoon to scoop out the pudding in thin slices. Dish the pudding slices into small bowls. Pour the ginger syrup over and serve.

> **Substitution tip:** Substitute ⅔ cup brown sugar or regular granulated sugar for the palm sugar.

Crispy Banana Fritters *Chuối Chiên*

MAKES 6 FRITTERS • PREP TIME: 7 MINUTES • COOK TIME: 15 MINUTES

Banana fritters are a common street food throughout the country, especially in the winter. Ripe bananas are lightly flattened, coated in rice flour batter, and deep-fried. The heat from the sizzling oil makes the bananas meltingly tender and gives them an almost caramel-like sweetness. The thin golden-brown rice coat adds delicious contrasting crispiness. You can eat these fritters on their own, or serve with coconut cream or whipped cream and roasted sesame seeds.

1 cup rice flour

Pinch salt

2/3 cup water

6 short bananas (bananitos or Thai bananas)

Vegetable oil, for frying

½ cup coconut cream or whipped cream, for serving (optional)

¼ cup roasted sesame seeds, for serving (optional)

1. In a large bowl, mix the flour, salt, and water until smooth. Set aside.
2. Peel the bananas. Place them on a cutting board and lightly flatten them with a knife.
3. Pour the oil into a small saucepan to a depth of about 1½ inches. Heat over medium heat until the oil reaches 350°F. (You can check the temperature by dipping a chopstick or a fork into the oil. If the oil sizzles, it's ready.)
4. Dip a banana into the batter and fry it immediately so the batter doesn't slide off. Fry until one side is golden, then flip and fry until the other side is golden. Transfer the fritter to a paper towel to drain. Repeat with the rest of the bananas.

5. Serve immediately while the fritters are still warm and crispy. Top with coconut cream and sesame seeds if desired.

> *Ingredient tip:* Choose bananas that are medium ripe or slightly overripe for this recipe.
>
> *Cooking tip:* I usually fry two fritters at a time in a small pan. If you fry more than one fritter, make sure the temperature remains at 350°F. Lower temperatures can result in soft or oily fritters.

Panna Cotta With Fresh Passion Fruit Juice *nna C ta Chanh Dây*

SERVES 4 • PREP TIME: 5 MINUTES + 4 HOURS TO CHILL • COOK TIME: 5 MINUTES

Passion fruit is called "vine lemon" in Vietnamese. It has a sour taste like lemon, but it's sweeter and has an irresistible aroma of honey, mint, and clementine. It's intense but pleasant. Passion fruit juice is among the most popular drinks in restaurants here. Also, it's a perfect match for Western desserts like ice cream, cheesecake, and mousse, to "tropicalize" these desserts and make them a refreshing treat for the summer. I came up with this simple variation of classic panna cotta when passion fruit was in season and I wanted to try something different. It's yummy and very easy to make. The vibrant honey-yellow color of passion fruit juice makes this a treat for the eyes as well as the taste buds.

2 tablespoons water

2 tablespoons gelatin powder

2½ cups heavy cream

3½ tablespoons milk

3½ tablespoons sugar

5 passion fruit

1. Put the water in a bowl and sprinkle the gelatin powder over it. Let sit for 5 minutes.

2. In a saucepan, whisk the cream, milk, and sugar until the sugar dissolves. Bring to a simmer over medium heat, then remove the pan from the heat.

3. Stir the gelatin into the saucepan until the gelatin dissolves, then strain the mixture into a bowl.

4. Pour the mixture into four cups, bowls, or molds. Refrigerate for at least 4 hours to set.

5. Cut the passion fruit in half. Use a spoon to scrape the juice and seeds over the panna cotta and serve.

***Ingredient tip:** Choose ripe passion fruit, which are dark purple. Light purple and green skins indicate underripe fruits that can be very sour. Passion fruit get sweeter if you keep them at room temperature for a few days until the skin shrinks and shrivels up. Some passion fruit are more sour than others. If you find yours too sour, you can add some honey or sugar to the juice and mix it before adding to the panna cotta.*

***Serving tip:** Alternatively, if you want to unmold the panna cotta upside-down on a plate, make sure to grease the molds or cups with butter first. Before serving, dip each mold in warm water for a minute and then run a knife around the edge before inverting it on a plate.*

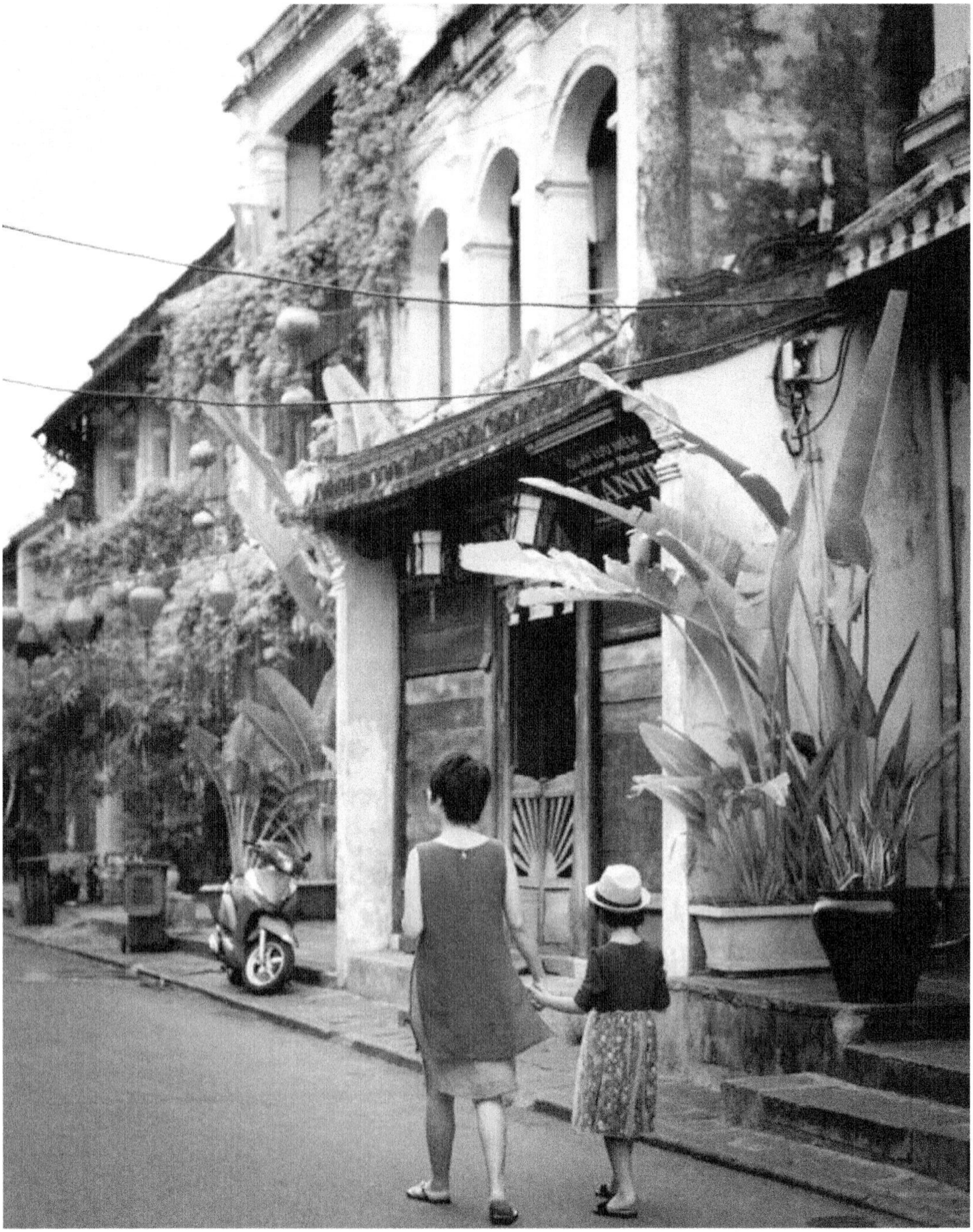

Quick Vietnamese Glossary

bánh — rice-based sweet treats
bánh mì — wheat bánh
bún — rice vermicelli
cá cơm — anchovy
cháo — porridge
chè — slow-cooked puddinglike desserts
cơm — rice
cuốn — rolls
gỏi — salad
mắm — fermented preserved anchovy, shrimp, or crab paste
nộm — salad
nước — *mắm* fish sauce
p/tở — noodle soup
quẩy — Chinese fried breadsticks/doughnuts
rau răm — Vietnamese coriander or Vietnamese mint
Tết — Vietnamese New Year

Printed in Dunstable, United Kingdom